THE PRIMARY TEACHER

The Primary Teacher:

The Role of the Educator and the Purpose of Primary Education

Edited by

Cedric Cullingford

CASSELL

Cassell Educational Limited
Artillery House
Artillery Row
London SW1P 1RT

First published 1989

British Library Cataloguing in Publication Data
The primary teacher: the role of the educator and the
  purpose of primary education.
  1. Primary schools. Teaching
  I. Cullingford, Cedric
  372.11′02

  ISBN 0–304–31790–X
     0–304–31791–8 (pbk)

Typeset by Input Typesetting Ltd, London
Printed and bound in Great Britain by
Biddles Ltd, Guildford and King's Lynn

Last digit is print no: 9 8 7 6 5 4 3 2 1

Contents

Notes on the Contributors

Kate Ashcroft worked as a primary teacher in Avon and Somerset before being appointed as senior lecturer in the Social Psychology of Education at Oxford Polytechnic in 1984. She became principal lecturer responsible for the development of the BEd course, before being appointed to her present post as BEd/DipHE course leader at Westminster College, Oxford, in 1988.

Hilary Burgess is a senior lecturer in Education at Newman and Westhill College, Birmingham. Previously she worked as a primary school teacher in ILEA and Coventry Education Authority. She has written upon the primary curriculum, case study research in the primary school, methods of assessment, and women and careers.

Cedric Cullingford is head of the Department of Primary Education at Brighton Polytechnic. His books include *Children and Television* and *Parents, Teachers and Schools*.

Andrew Pollard has taught across the primary age range, particularly in infant schools. He is now Reader in Education at Bristol Polytechnic and director of the Redland Centre for Primary Education. His books include *The Social World of the Primary School* and *Reflective Teaching in the Primary School*.

Gary Thomas has worked as a teacher, an educational psychologist and a lecturer in Education. He has most recently worked as senior educational psychologist and tutor for advanced training in educational psychology at University College, London, and is now senior lecturer in special education at Oxford Polytechnic. His books include *Planning for Special Needs* and *Tackling Learning Difficulties*.

Norman Thomas was formerly Her Majesty's Chief Inspector for Primary Schools and, more recently, the chairman of the group that produced the ILEA report on improving primary schools. He was adviser to the Parliamentary Select Committee in the study on primary education. He was a member of the Task Group on Assessment and Testing.

Edwina Vold is associate professor and chair of the Department of Professional Studies at Indiana University of Pennsylvania, Indiana, Pa. She co-authored *Multicultural Education*, a resource book. Her previous appointments include a period as associate director of the Teacher Corps Project at the University of Wisconsin, and she was associate professor at Norfolk State University, Norfolk, Virginia, where she directed a multicultural teacher education project. Dr Vold is an active consultant throughout the United States.

Preface

The times we live in almost always feel unstable when we compare them with the past. Instead of the security of observable slow development we feel the insecurity of constant harassment and conflicting ideas. Whilst this might be a common feeling, there is little doubt that in the world of education we are going through a period not only of the instability of questioning, but the institutionalizing of such instability. Not only are many of the given values of culture being questioned, but bureaucracies are being set up to question them. The values of the school and their purpose and role in society are the subject not so much of scrutiny, but of assertions, not so much of an examining of evidence, but of searching for support to justify assertions.

At the most profound level such instability affects teachers. Their status in society, their role in relation to parents, and their responsibilities are all questioned. They are undermined by the assumptions that produce a national curriculum or teacher appraisal. Many of the statements made about education – so often negative – are implied, or blatant, criticisms of teachers. And yet teachers are what any education system depends on; not rules or regulations, criteria or tests. It is through the individual personalities of teachers, their sense of purpose, their relationship to children, and their understanding of how they learn, that all real change takes place.

In all the universal questions about education – who do we blame for the faults of society; do we believe that education can change society; indeed, is society changeable? – the central issues rest on the teachers. And yet this fact is easily forgotten; those who criticize do not always realize the implications of what they are saying; those who defend are not always very articulate.

This book is addressed to the central issues of primary/elementary education. All questions circle around the role of the teacher.

Introduction

The shadow of the National Curriculum and testing falls across all the pages of this book, but like all shadows it is caused by something more substantial. The debates about the national curriculum, the sense of threat and defensiveness, the assertions about 'raising standards', are usually unsupported by evidence, and do not always tackle the central issues. The arguments about the control of the curriculum and the autonomy of schools focus attention on the central issues of primary education and the role of primary teachers.

Arguments about the content of the curriculum have been with us for a number of years, and will remain with us for years to come, long after the more ephemeral ones concerning the implementation of the Education Act. There is a sense of inevitability about the relationship between the social climate and its manifestation in political terms. A number of chapters in this book place these issues in a more complete context. The debates about the national curriculum highlight the question of the purpose of primary schools, and the control over what children should be learning. For we know that there is a gap between the superficial idea of a curriculum consisting of defined subjects which are 'delivered' to receiving audiences, and the actual learning which takes place in a more subtle way.

The debate about the control of the curriculum reveals how little is understood about the nature of primary schools, and how little people *wish* to understand. Despite many research studies referred to in this book, which analyse the institutions and the people in them, the ostensible aims and the hidden curriculum, there is still embedded in the general debate a notion of the primary school as a simple, even simple-minded, institution. The curriculum is still described in terms of outcomes, in the examination system which dominates secondary schools. Primary schools are still questioned for the subtlety of their teaching methods and their view of the process of children's education. There is even some exasperation expressed that primary schools are concerned with individuals' learning rather than the results of learning, with what is called a 'bottom-up' view of the curriculum rather than a 'top-down' model.

Any concern with a national curriculum, therefore, draws attention to the nature of primary schools; the ability of the individual teacher to organize children's learning, and the autonomy of the individual schools. It is through primary schools that essential educational questions need to be addressed. Their success cannot be measured in terms of exam results; formalized testing will not necessarily give us insight into the learning process.

The question of the control of the curriculum will affect primary teachers in a number of ways. The position of parents and the community, the demands of national testing, especially in relation to topic work and the whole question of appraisal, all put the professional nature of the job under a new scrutiny. The implications of a national curriculum can already be observed. In France, for example, where there is a national curriculum already in place, the teachers feel more secure for having a curriculum imposed upon them[1]. For the French, 'teaching style' is a more simple matter, the passing on of a body of knowledge rather than an attempt to develop and socialize a child, questioned by parents, headteachers and inspectors. English teachers take on far more responsibility. Far more is expected of them[2]. And yet the French teachers appear to have more support from other professionals and more respect from parents. English teachers have wide-ranging responsibilities together with individual notions of pedagogy. A powerful impact of the national curriculum will be changing the level of demand made on teachers. This could be a great loss, or a sensible accommodation.

The national curriculum has drawn attention to external pressures on primary schools. But for some time it has not been realistic to picture primary schools as cut off from their clientele, as secret places about which little is known. As many chapters of this book make clear, the traditional view of a primary classroom, safe within the four walls, no longer applies. There are not only subtle demands from outside – on additions to the curriculum like health, or industry or computing – but obvious intrusions in the shape of other people, as well as whole school policies. Whilst the earlier chapters focus on the nature of the curriculum and its impact on the teacher's job, the essential and lasting focus is on the need for the new professional to understand the changing nature of teaching in primary schools.

Primary schools are complex places, complex in the interaction between internal and external demands, and in the relationships between heads and teaching staff, between teachers and children. There are few institutions with which one can compare them. But the nature of teaching is an even more complex activity than has been generally recognized, even if we tend to think about it in simplistic terms. The ability to respond to many individual children, according to their temperament and mood as well as abilities and motivation, is one of the most intellectually challenging tasks in existence. For those who have taught in universities as well as in infant classrooms there is no doubt that the younger the age range the more demanding is the task, not just in terms of emotional responsiveness but the ability to judge the circumstances exactly. The teacher not only needs to know a wide range of subjects, but needs to understand how children respond to them. She needs to know how to convey the excitement of learning through a variety of different techniques. Compared with organizing a classroom, teaching in higher education is intellectually easy. [Note: for simplicity, the use of female gender for teacher and male gender for child has been adopted throughout the book.]

The subtlety that a teacher faces with young children is that learning is not a simple matter of will or rejection of the will to learn. The emotional needs from which children derive their motivation have not yet been narrowed or channelled into academic exercises. Teachers are aware of the impact of the different styles on individual pupils, but are also aware that their responses cannot be manipulated in terms of different socio-economic backgrounds. And yet the changing nature of society makes it increasingly necessary for the teacher to take account of cultural differences. The ideal of education for equality is even more important, indeed obvious, in a multicultural society which affects all people whatever their immediate daily circumstances.

Issues of gender, race and culture, which derive from broad distinctions themselves, point to the complexities of individual differences. But they also draw attention to the emotional pressures on teachers, to the fact that education includes questions of personal integrity as well as the delivery of the curriculum. The tensions of the personal and political arguments that surround multicultural studies versus anti-racism themselves reveal how volatile is the subject. Teachers find themselves not only working out how to respond to the changing nature of their clientele but given conflicting advice on how to do so. The problem is that there are issues of learning so broad that they are beyond the scope of this book. Teachers respond to a series of external factors which are not just a matter of personal organization but which challenge the ways in which teachers think of their job. Matters such as other people in the classroom, or the ethos of school, make an emotional impact, which is surrounded by the broader question of how children respond in terms of ability, attitude or culture. Although this book focuses particularly on the role of the teacher, the other issues are implied even when they are not directly addressed.

It is this awareness of the teacher's difficulties and the subtleties of a teacher's role that this book celebrates. It explores many of the issues which define what it is like to be a teacher. It shows how the job has been changing, is changing and will change in many ways, and yet how certain issues remain central. We know that the impact a teacher can make is enormous, if incalculable. We also know that this is a truth not generally recognized. We know that some schools perform better than others, and that some teachers perform better than others. It is the nature of such differences the book sets out to explore, both to define quality and celebrate the achievements of primary teachers.

In the end we are concerned with the education of children. To primary teachers the 'raising of standards' is no political war cry but a daily concern that varies from individual to individual. It is a concern that cannot be met in isolation but one which involves many people. Although the book is concerned with teachers, the children have their chapters too. For whilst the debate about the curriculum centres in the end on the nature of teaching, the essential question will always be about the nature of learning; not what is given to children but what children receive.

REFERENCES

(1) Broadfoot, P. and Osborn, M., with Gilly, M. and Paillet, A. 'Teachers' conceptions of their professional responsibility: some international comparisons'. *Comparative Education*, **23** (3), 287–302, 1987.
(2) Cullingford, C. *Parents, Teachers and Schools*. London: R. Royce (Cassell), 1985.

Chapter 1

The Teacher and the Purpose of Primary Education

Cedric Cullingford

There are some truths universally acknowledged but about which
little is done. It is an ancient wisdom, not confined to the Jesuits,
that the essential character of people, their attitudes and motivation, are formed in their early years. It is also a new wisdom,
reiterated in many research studies, that the earliest experiences
of childhood and their subsequent development give the basis
both for ability and what the individual does about it. The only
question is whether the parents and other adults are the most
important influence, or whether the initial experiences of schooling have an equally powerful effect. What is not in question is
the understanding that the earlier years of education are more
formative than the later ones[1].

And yet, no amount of evidence seems to make a difference to
the way in which primary education, in the broadest sense, is
regarded. Adults look back with self-conscious familiarity on their
experiences at secondary school and in higher education, when
they were more aware of what they were learning, and less aware
of being taught. Over the gulf of the years lies an almost deliberate
forgetfulness that makes the experience of primary schools seem
like an alien territory. It is far easier to look back, with the
hindsight of more recently acquired knowledge, than to grasp the
developing thoughts of one's younger self exploring the environment with precision and panache. Our later point of view can be
singular and egocentric; as if we become less and less aware of
our dependence on the past.

One of the clearest signs of the general lack of understanding
of the importance of primary schools is the misunderstanding of

the role of teachers in them. It is a universal problem. In many countries elementary teachers undergo a completely separate system of training, both shorter and less rigorous than that of their secondary counterparts, as if it were less demanding to teach younger children[2]. Their very expertise as teachers is not rated as highly as the ability to know a particular subject well[3]. This distinction between recognition of the importance of good teaching and expertise in one part of the curriculum is shared by the children themselves. By the time they leave primary school, children believe that it is only a preparation for the important events to come; that secondary school is more significant and that all education leads to the pursuit of qualifications for jobs[4]. The dominating difficulty in the purpose of primary schools is the fact that 'knowing' is rated more highly than 'teaching', despite the importance of the latter and its equally intimate connection with 'learning'.

The distinct role of the primary school, often seen in terms of conveying essential skills – reading and writing and arithmetic – as well as the ability to mix in the society of others, is itself being eroded. We note the growing recognition of the part that parents can play. The primary teacher is therefore no longer seen as the only expert on whom the parent must wait so that the child can be instructed. Nor is the school any longer seen as the place where all the deficiencies of home can be compensated[5]. The recognition of the more subtle skills of learning, through relationships and through motivation, through the home and pre-school experiences, means that the singular purpose of primary schools is less easily defined.

The erosion of the traditional position of the primary school teacher also takes place at the point where children move on. There have been many experiments with middle schools, on the grounds that the transition from primary school to secondary school, from generalism to specialism, cannot be handled by the primary schools themselves. From the Primary Survey of 1978 onwards the government has been concerned to make the primary teacher more of a specialist, playing the role of consultant to colleagues as well as handling the complexities of a large class[6]. The training of primary school teachers is not only marked by the growing number of those who enter the profession after a specialized first degree followed by a postgraduate certificate, but the demand that *all* should have at least two years of a 'subject study'. A simplified notion of the curriculum was first evident in the criteria laid down on teacher training, long before the national framework. On the one hand, the primary teacher is seen to be more dependent on, and answerable to, the parents and the community. On the other hand, the primary teacher is defined as a specialist, not as a specialist teacher, but as a specialist in a particular area of the curriculum.

One of the reasons for this conflict in attitudes derives from the very image that primary schools have tended to project, whether they liked it or not. For the 'general public' the virtues of primary schools have been associated with comfortable stability, where children's happiness has been deemed more important than their academic advance, as if the two were in opposition to each other. The desire to make children feel at home in strange circumstances, with other children, and to foster in them a sense of personal well-being, has given primary schools a particular ethos. The children themselves contrast their sense of the comfort of the primary school against that of the bustle and demands of the secondary[7]. At best such a sense of security suggests that children's well-being is fostered in a variety of ways, that they are free to explore ideas, to ask questions and fulfil their own talents. At worst, such emphasis on security can seem to outsiders as wasteful, not making enough demands and not matching appropriate tasks to the ability of children.

One of the abiding concerns in the educational system generally is what Hargreaves calls the 'cult of individualism'[8]. At the primary schools this can be projected as 'child centred' in the sense of a belief in the autonomy of the individual child and his innate ability to be creative and imaginative. The problem with such a view of children's own capacities is that it leads to the assumption that schools can do little to compensate for the problems of society or the child's home background[9]. If a child is an autonomous learner it can be argued that each has to find his own way of learning, at the same time as adapting to the many rules of behaviour, both explicit and implied, that the school presents. This can be difficult for children. If we observe children in a primary school, noting their experiences rather than being caught up in the demands of our own teaching, it is clear that from the child's point of view some of the impressions of school are not part of the school's intentions.

It is impossible for schools to make everything explicit but there are many ambiguities for children. Despite the emphasis on achievement and concentration, children spend a significant proportion of the day waiting for things to happen. They are puzzled by the relationship between work and play. Play is constantly being redefined, as something which is a prelude to work, something which interferes with work, as a form of learning. Play is something done at particular times, and seldom if ever by teachers. Play is what young children do; work is done for the teacher[10]. Children begin to develop an attitude towards work which derives from these impressions, and begin to assume that it is those comparatively brief periods of 'work' that most matter. This also means that children accept that waiting for the next task to be presented to them is an essential part of school. Children wait while the classroom is organized, and sometimes look for things to do, volunteering help – 'Shall I shut the door'? – or doing some covert reading or talking. Waiting includes keeping an eye on the teacher to be ready for that moment when she gives an instruction to which they have to pay attention. Children wait for tasks without questioning the purpose of what they are doing. The setting of tasks and the creation of order does not imply that the children are learning in every moment.

Given the extraordinarily difficult demands on primary school teachers, and given the traditionally bare resources devoted to one classroom and thirty children, it is not surprising that the experience of some children can be as seemingly purposeless as in the picture just given. But the real problem for the many creative and talented classteachers is to harness a sense of purpose both in individual children and in the schools as a whole.

Primary teachers have not been helped by some of the mythologies about school. Many of the associations fostered by the Plowden report[11] seem gratifying, but have not really enabled teachers to define their own sense of purpose. We know about the capacities of children, but cannot assume that their talents will reveal themselves the moment they are given the opportunity[12]. The Plowden report emphasized the need to nurture the personal growth of individual children rather than more formal aspects of learning, and directed attention away from the school to the child's own environment[13]. But this was not a precise shift towards the involvement of parents, or towards planning specific ways in which those outside school could help children. Classrooms remained the same; they were only seen differently.

Such optimism about childhood innocence meant that teachers were not supposed to be dogmatic about knowledge, and could not impose on the children. Instead they were to let children acquire knowledge from personal experience, and to create conditions in which they could do so. Such an account necessarily simplifies some of the arguments from the Plowden report but it does suggest that at the core of the report lay the belief that the role of the primary teacher was more to support than to direct. The teachers should provide a rich environment in which children would flourish of their own accord[14].

The problem with such a Plowdenesque view of primary education is that it does not define the purpose or the role of the teachers, or, indeed, the nature of what the children are supposed to learn.

The popularity of the Plowden report gave impetus to the idea that social and emotional development was more important than intellectual achievement. There was bound to be a reaction against such a perceived position, and this then led to a polarization of the views about the purpose of primary schools, especially in the early years[15]. In simple terms schools are supposed either to provide a secure environment for learning or teach the children to do well academically[16]. The desire to lay down a centralized curriculum, with objectives of achievement in terms of knowledge, which can be tested, is to be seen, since the 1978 Primary Survey, as an almost inevitable reaction. The wish to order what proportion of time should be spent on 'core' subjects and other parts of the curriculum is not just a determination to impose control but a desire from outside to understand what goes on within the classroom. Individualized learning is subtle. It is easier for parents and others to understand progress in terms of subjects.

Primary schools have not been helped in articulating their sense of purpose and distinctive ethos by these conflicts between different views of their role; whether they are concerned with the process of the developing child or with the outcomes of attainment as measured against pre-set criteria.

There are many ways in which primary schools can be acknowledged for the importance of what they are doing, and be encouraged to develop the gifts of individual children, always acknowledging that their achievement could be much greater. The sense of autonomy, or freedom from imposed constraints, can be used to advantage. At best, this means that teachers can take risks, can go beyond the idea of an allotted syllabus, and explore those questions that children most want to explore, the meaning of what they are doing and the meaning of their lives in relation to others. At worst, the autonomy of the schools can lead to a lack of enthusiasm, a satisfaction with keeping children happy, making sure that there is no disturbance in the secret enclosures of the classroom.

The teacher in the traditional classroom, however, faces dangers as well as opportunities. Ostensibly, freedom from outside constraints and outside contacts can mean that there is no need to explain or articulate what is going on. Teachers rarely see other's classrooms, or visit other schools. They are nearly always in their own classroom. They are not forced by colleagues to define or analyse what they are doing. Many of the most impressive teachers, sensitive to and responding to individual children's needs, are not given an opportunity to explain what they are doing. This is one of the reasons why there is so much misunderstanding about the demands and subtleties of their role. One of the most creative uses of in-service courses is to enable teachers to work alongside others, to share their experiences and to define what they observe.

There are, however, some outside pressures which might define the work of the primary school teacher more clearly, and might, ironically, lead to greater recognition of the importance of her role. The suggestion of the Task Group on Assessment and Testing that teachers should meet to discuss both their own and national criteria in relation to each other could lead to more awareness and communication about what children are learning, and how[17].

Teacher appraisal is also a result of a developing concern for accountability and evaluation; firstly for institutions and then for individuals. It could mean little more than a diversion of resources into larger bureaucracies, with more inspectors rather than more teachers, but it could also lead to changes in which the complex skills of teaching are recognized by others. Teachers have always been evaluated, whether at an anecdotal level or in formal interviews for promotion. But judgements will become more formally based on evidence. This will require some very complex changes, with people being trained how to carry out 'clinical observation' and how to give advice. Formality in assessing the performance of the teacher also implies a commitment to staff development.

Appraisal is not just a question of removing or chastening the weaker teacher, but after diagnosing what is weak, finding the means to rectify the weakness. New forms of teacher appraisal should lead to a greater concern for the professional development of teachers, and therefore a greater awareness of what it is that makes teachers successful.

When talking about 'values' it is easy to be vague, contradictory or abstract. But 'purposes' are often implicit, especially in primary schools, where the understanding of children's capacities for learning can be joined by an awareness of the intricate skills of teaching. All the subtle changes that are taking place within the school community, from the greater involvement of parents to the demands of the national curriculum, will have an impact on the ways that teachers perform. There is a sense of inevitability about these changes because they are the result of conclusions reached from different points of view.

The recognition of the role of parents in schools, for example, is shared for opposing political reasons. From one point of view the involvement of parents means an opening up of the school, a responsiveness to society. From another it means greater accountability to the clients and the community. Teacher appraisal is seen by some as a means of making distinctions and demarcations between teachers, and removing any bad ones. By others it is seen as enhancing professional development. The role of a subject consultant might appear from one point of view the result of a standard and agreed curriculum. From another it is the manifestation of the natural enthusiasm of a teacher for her subject, whatever the subject, a specialism which conveys the excitement of the quality of learning for its own sake.

Primary school teachers constantly need to redefine their purpose because of the ambiguities with which they are confronted, between the individual 'holistic' nature of learning and the imposition of a set curriculum leading to assessment. Relying on the assumption that children are innately gifted and merely need the right environment for their gifts to manifest themselves is no more helpful than defining the body of knowledge they must possess, according to criteria worked out by age. For there is much more to what a primary school teacher does than either minding children or directing what they should learn. The paradox for teachers is the fact that the more they define their professional role, as people able to help others make better use of knowledge, the less their status is likely to be understood[18]. The position of teachers in some countries which possess an agreed curriculum seems more secure in the eyes of the general public. But it is in the more subtle understanding of the process of education that primary schools find their central role.

As visible entities primary schools are easily recognized as distinct. But they are not uniform. There are many distinctions between the style of individual teachers and the sense of purpose in the school as a whole. The success or failure of children depends on the kinds of motivation shared by the staff and generated by them[19]. It derives from a sense of purpose rather than a matter of what is added to the curriculum.

The purpose of primary education is not easily summarized. It is difficult to convey to those who demand that purposes are expressed in terms of curriculum outcomes symbolized by the examination system. It is also hard to express to parents and children who agree that the real purpose of education is the preparation for jobs. No amount of sentiment about schools will help either the teachers or the children. But the central concern with the individual child is a motivating factor whose potential has hardly been realized. The awareness of the role of parents, and the concern with what happens subsequently, are both helpful in defining more clearly the particular concern with the whole that primary schools convey. Drawing attention to the dilemmas should focus attention on how best we can define the means we have for helping children learn.

REFERENCES AND NOTES

(1) Wells, G. *Language Development in the Pre-School Years*. Cambridge, UK: Cambridge University Press, 1985; Richman, N., Stevenson, T. and Graham, P. J. *Pre-School to School: A Behavioural Study*. London: Academic Press, 1982.
(2) One recent Secretary of State for Education could not understand why the education of a teacher in a first school should be the same in length as that for a teacher in a secondary school; he thought they needed only half the time.
        Examples of the distinction between the types of training can be taken from many different parts of the world, from China to Peru.
(3) *See* Chapter 7.
(4) Cullingford, C. ' "I suppose learning your tables could help you

get a job": children's views on the purpose of schools'. *Education 3–13*, **14** (2), 41–6, 1986.

(5) *See* Cullingford, C. *Parents, Teachers and Schools*: London: R. Royce, 1985.

(6) HMI. *Primary Survey*. London: HMSO, 1978.

(7) Cullingford, C. 'School rules and children's attitudes to discipline'. *Educational Research*, **30** (1), 3–8, 1988.

(8) Hargreaves, D. H. 'A sociological critique of individualism in education'. *British Journal of Education Studies*, **28** (3), 187, 1980.

(9) *See* Sharp, R. and Green, A. *Educational and Social Control*. London: Routledge & Kegan Paul, 1975, p. 82.

(10) King, R. *All Things Bright and Beautiful? A Sociological Study of Infants Classrooms*. Chichester, UK: Wiley, 1978.

(11) Department of Education and Science. *Children and Their Primary Schools* (Plowden report). London: HMSO, 1967.

(12) The capacity of children is nearly always greater than the performance; work with the many cases of 'exceptional' children shows how great this is. The literature on children's capabilities in a number of fields is growing and can be found in journals such as *Child Development*.

(13) Bassett, G. W. *Innovation in Primary Education*. London: Wiley, 1980.

(14) Blenkin, G. A. and Kelly, A. V. *The Primary Curriculum*. London: Harper & Row, 1981.

(15) Tamburrini, J. 'New directions in nursery school education'. In Richards, C. *New Directions in Primary Education*. Lewes, UK: Falmer Press, 1982.

(16) Taylor, P., Exon, G. and Holley, B. *A Study of Nursery Education*. London: Evans Methuen, 1972.

(17) DES. *Task Group on Assessment and Testing: A Report*. By P. J. Black *et al*. London: HMSO, 1988.

(18) Hoyle, E. 'The professionalisation of teachers: a paradox'. *British Journal of Educational Studies*, **30** (2) 161–71, 1982.

(19) Mortimore, P., Sammons, P., Stoll, L., Lewis, D. and Ecob, R. *School Matters: The Junior Years*. Wells, UK: Open Books, 1988.

Chapter 2

The Primary Curriculum: The Example of Mathematics

Hilary Burgess

EDITOR'S COMMENT

The word curriculum, is of course, a Humpty Dumpty word. It can be used in a variety of ways.

> 'When I use a word', said Humpty Dumpty, 'I use it in any way I please'.
> 'The question is', said Alice, 'whether you *can* use words in that way'.
> 'The question is', said Humpty Dumpty, 'who is to be master, that's all'.

Sometimes it is used to cover *all* that is going on in schools, obvious or hidden. Sometimes it is used to mean defined subject content clearly delivered. Such ambiguity means that many of the debates about a national curriculum are carried out with assertions rather than evidence.

Nowhere is such uncertainty about fact so clear as in the assumptions made about the 'core' curriculum. For years the assertion that primary schools were not teaching enough Maths and English was taken as a self-evident truth. And yet, we know from all the surveys that these subjects dominated the school day – to the detriment of other subjects, as Her Majesty's Inspectors of Schools (HMI) observed in the 1978 Primary Survey. Just as far fewer schools took on the principles of the Plowden report than its general impact might suggest, so far fewer schools were extending the narrow and traditional curriculum in new directions than might have seemed to be the case.

The gap between rhetoric and reality in the delivery of the curriculum is made clear in this chapter. There are several important themes which have a great deal of relevance to the whole of the curriculum. The amount of time spent by children in waiting for things to happen, and the questionable analysis when children's learning is defined in terms of 'time on task', are just two themes of which we need to be aware. The actual use of time is clearly a far more complex matter than it seems at first glance. There are already certain subjects which are clearly seen as important, and central. But the crucial matter is what children think and make of them. ∎   (C.C.)

Understanding the curriculum of the primary school is a highly complex activity. It is complex because the primary curriculum is about far more than simply the content of the subjects to be taught; it is also imbued with a range of assumptions concerning teacher ideology about the ways in which pupils learn, the teacher–pupil relationship, the teacher's role and a whole set of notions about what children should be taught and expected to learn. The primary curriculum, therefore, generates a great deal of discussion and debate which may be reflected in educational reports and documents presented by Her Majesty's Inspectors of Schools (HMI) and the Department of Education and Science (DES). The present preoccupation of educationalists is with 'achievement'[1], while earlier commentators promoted the 'child centred' philosophy[2] and encouraged learning through activity and experience. The discussion about monitoring, assessment and accountability was initiated in the 1970s and is now, in the 1980s, consolidated by HMI discussion documents upon the curriculum.

Such an approach gains momentum with the Education Reform Act which provides for the establishment of a national curriculum comprising core and foundation subjects. The four key stages for the assessment of pupils are at the ages of 7, 11, 14 and 16 years. Recommendations for programmes of study and specified attainment targets in mathematics and science are proposed[3]. The heavy emphasis upon control of academic achievement is also highlighted by the provision of City Technical Colleges which will have a specialized curriculum. Intimations of a centrally controlled curriculum have been apparent for some time in HMI[4] discussion on the content of the curriculum. For example, the organization of curriculum content at secondary school level is praised[5]:

> In secondary schools subjects are well established as a convenient and familiar way of organising learning, and in their selection of

subjects they try to ensure for their pupils a broad, balanced and useful education . . . one of their strengths lies in subjects well taught by staff with specialised training and experience.

However, the view expressed by HMI of primary schooling is tempered by discussion which focuses upon the disadvantages at this level of class and curriculum organization. While they are in agreement about young children needing 'sustained contact with one teacher' they go on to say[6]:

The main disadvantage of this system is that few individual teachers can be so expert in every part of the curriculum as to ensure that the special features of each subject or area make their full contribution to the education of the older children.

Primary school curriculum organization is also criticized when Topic Work is discussed. Here, HMI recognize that such an approach will maintain the interest of pupils but comment[7]:

it can be difficult to ensure that there is sufficient progression and continuity, particularly for older children, in the work in each area covered by a topic and it may be easier to plan progression if some of the work is organised as separate subjects.

An analysis of the curriculum which focuses upon subject divisions is reinforced by later HMI discussion papers which are organized under subject headings. Debate which centres around what 'ought to be' or 'should be' included as part of the primary curriculum does not examine what is really happening inside primary schools in the 1980s.

A major difficulty about understanding primary schooling is concerned with the way teachers view their roles. Within the secondary school, teachers are specialists within their own subject or area and, therefore, their professional role is largely concerned with imparting curriculum knowledge to pupils. Within the primary school, teachers give precedence to knowledge of pupils rather than curriculum knowledge. As Robin Alexander states, primary school teachers have an 'ideological commitment to "child not curriculum" '[8]. The focus when teaching the primary curriculum, therefore, is upon 'the child' not 'the subject'; a view which was brought to prominence by the publication of the Plowden report.

Although the ideals of Plowden, such as a child-centred curriculum and learning through experience and activity, may have become part of primary school teacher ideology, they are not always reflected in practice. Indeed, Brian Simon[9] questions whether the so-called primary school revolution is myth or reality and suggests that recent research[10] reveals that the Plowden ideals were not taken up by the majority of primary school teachers. The complexity of the primary curriculum cannot be understood, therefore, through an analysis of the subject areas which are taught. It involves an examination of what both teachers and pupils do; how lessons are organized, how the curriculum is selected, and how those areas which are deemed important, such as mathematics, are given a particular status and relevance through the allocation of time. This chapter focuses upon some of the major curriculum issues in the primary school, such as curriculum planning and development, the matching of pupil ability to lesson activity, the problems of class organization, and the ways in which both teachers and pupils use their time during lessons. Each of these issues has been discussed in some depth by a range of educational commentators. For example, Campbell[11] provides detailed discussion on school-based curriculum development and examines the role of curriculum consultants and the participation of other teachers in the process of curriculum development. The influence of individual members of staff upon the school curriculum is also highlighted by Pollard[12], who examines how teachers may use strategies to manipulate the implementation or non-implementation of school curriculum policy.

Activities inside the classroom, such as the process of teaching and learning, are constantly being reviewed by educationalists. Indeed, the concept of 'match', which was initially focused upon by HMI in their report *Primary Education in England*[13], has become a prominent issue in the 1980s. HMI considered that while teachers were able to match activities to pupil ability in core curriculum areas such as mathematics and language, other areas were not sufficiently 'matched' to pupil ability. Further research[14] has considered some of the difficulties which teachers face when attempting to match pupils to a range of activities and the role that assessment can have in this process.

An analysis of the use of time by both teachers and pupils is a major way in which the activities of the primary curriculum can be understood. Time, used as a conceptual tool, can explain numerous features of classroom life and it is also the medium through which both teachers and pupils plan their activities. For example, some pupil activities may be encouraged by teachers through their definitions of appropriate behaviour within and beyond the classroom[15]. How teachers and pupils use their time during a school day, therefore, may be studied as a means of understanding 'curriculum practice' in the primary school.

Detailed portraits of what actually happens in primary schools are relatively rare[16], and their worth in developing our understanding of school activities is recognized by few researchers apart from sociologists. In this chapter, what actually happens in the teaching of one curriculum area, mathematics, will be used to examine curriculum practice. The concept of time is used to both contextualize and link the themes across the primary curriculum. The example of mathematics is taken from a case study in one school. The case study was conducted in a primary school which I called Elm Park Primary[17], and focused upon the way in which teachers defined and redefined the mathematics curriculum in their classroom practice. The major methods of social investigation used were informal interviews and observation in classrooms. Use was also made of documentary evidence such as the mathematics syllabus and other papers on mathematics, texts and wall displays. The concept of time will be used to raise questions about the primary curriculum, in a similar way to that in which Delamont and Galton[18] used time to analyse the secondary curriculum.

Time is an overriding factor where school activities are concerned. For example, curriculum emphasis is given to the subjects upon which most time is spent; pupil activity is often regulated by a timetable; and teachers use their time within the school and classroom in specific ways. Through the medium of time, therefore, it will be possible to examine in depth classroom activities. Discussion will centre around ways in which teachers utilize time in the organization of their daily mathematics lessons; how revision within mathematics has an annual and termly programme – a use of time which is linked to the way primary school children learn; and the implications for the hidden curriculum of mathematical education. However, we turn first to an analysis of time within the school timetable.

TIME IN THE TIMETABLE

There are few primary schools in the 1980s where classes of children adhere to a rigidly constructed timetable. However, in many schools there are timetables for assemblies, breaks and lunch hours, the beginning and end of the school day, times for games and PE in the hall, the use of television and computer, and – where a specialist teacher is available – music. Indeed, in studying this list of fixed 'times' for various activities it is apparent that a school year, term, week and day are regulated and therefore provide a structure within which both pupils and teachers operate. How, therefore, does the use of time affect the ways in which teachers implement the curriculum?

Within primary schools the daily classroom activities may be structured into small units of time. As Ronald King discovered while conducting research in infant schools[19]:

> The classroom was the physical setting for a profusion of activities. At first it was difficult to see the way these were structured. The timetable in each school controlled only the use of non-classrooms, such as the hall, television room, and maths workshop. The within classroom activities were to some extent structured around these, and around the dinner and playtime breaks. Every day was phased into small divisions of time. Mrs Pink's day began with coming into class time, followed by hanging up coats time, then news time, register time, getting ready for first activity time. Getting ready for milk time preceded milk time, which led to clearing away after milk time, and then going to the lavatory before play time. The day included singing time, washing hands before dinner time, and ended with story time, putting on coats time, and finally goodbye time.

The whole of these infants' days were structured into units of time when activities occurred. It was only after a period of observation that in fact the 'time' organization of the school day became obvious to Ronald King as his examination of the school timetables revealed very little. Indeed, the writers of the Select Committee Report argued that rigidly timetabled classes may result from the use of subject headings but do not provide sufficient information about what is actually taught.

The importance of the allocation of time to areas of learning is discussed within the report in some detail where the committee arrived at the conclusion that[20]:

> it is a myth that there is no differentiation of children's timetables in primary schools, though it is common for the timetable to be arranged by the class teacher subject to overriding decisions about the use of facilities shared between classes – like the hall or the micro-computer.

The major restriction, therefore, upon the timetable of a primary classroom is to do with the sharing of resources and extra space for particular activities rather than upon questions about what is to be taught. The select committee, though, did not consider that descriptions of classroom activities would be a useful way to describe the primary curriculum, as they comment[21]:

> although timetables are rarely haphazard, as a casual observer might suppose, they are too various to provide useful headings by which to analyse the curriculum; and even where a heading seems clear, what is actually taught is often more complex than the heading suggests.

It appears that the usefulness of timetables as a means of understanding what happens inside classrooms is, therefore, in doubt. Is the primary curriculum, then, too complex to encapsulate or group under a series of headings? In the recent past teachers have been criticized[22] for concentrating too much on the teaching of basics such as mathematics and language and providing insufficient match between pupils and other classroom activities. The prominence of mathematics teaching in the primary curriculum certainly provided a rich source of data for my research at Elm Park Primary. Indeed, the importance attached to the teaching of mathematics meant that a major portion of time was allocated each day. The teachers at Elm Park completed a weekly timetable showing where they taught mathematics and for how long each day. In almost every case, nearly one quarter of the teaching time each day was allocated to the teaching of mathematics. On all the timetables I received, the subject was taught during the morning sessions. A note on one of the timetables explained the timing of the lessons by saying 'mornings seem best for children'.

For the teachers at Elm Park, therefore, the timing of the lessons during the day as well as the length of the lessons played an important part in their teaching programme. The areas of the curriculum which the teachers considered to be the most important were taught during the time of day when children's learning was thought to be at a peak.

This timetable evidence was later verified during conversational interviews with the staff at Elm Park. Indeed, over this particular issue both the infant and junior teachers were in agreement. One infant teacher described her day as the mornings being the time when work on mathematics and language was conducted, while the afternoons were the time for 'messy' activities. She said:

> I love being messy with them as well. I like the messy activities which we do a lot of in the afternoon and I like to play with them

in the Wendy House . . . They are desperately wanting to read when they come to school. To them it has just been a page of hieroglyphics until you actually introduce them to reading. I was just talking to them this morning about it.

In this classroom time is divided into two distinct periods. Work on basic curriculum areas and class discussion which takes place in the morning and the 'messy' activities which might also involve playing in the Wendy House in the afternoon. Time within a junior classroom was also broken up, providing both routine and a 'time for practice' as a junior teacher commented on mathematics teaching:

> We do a lot of practice. In the mornings when they first come in, while I am doing the register and so on, they have work on the board to be doing a quick practice, what we call their quick practice books, which are marked and talked about, if I feel it needs it.

Such use of time during lessons has been described by Hargreaves, Hestor and Mellor[23] as an entry and settling down phase. Pollard develops this notion and discusses how an understanding of rules is an essential feature of classroom life. He argues that such rules are the result of tacit understandings and therefore ' "frame" the actions of both teacher and pupils'[24]. While behaviour is clearly defined the rule frame is high. The rule frame in Elm Park classrooms acted as a time when children settled quickly to work while the teacher was occupied with the activity of marking the register.

Accordingly, the amount of time allocated to the teaching of mathematics and the morning space on the timetable all emphasize the importance of mathematics teaching for the staff at Elm Park. These timetabling arrangements might be considered part of the hidden curriculum in that they signal to pupils messages about the status of mathematics as a subject compared with other subject areas. Also the use of morning sessions for the teaching of mathematics implies assumptions on the part of the teachers about children's cognitive processes in the transmission of some subjects and suggests that children are best able to learn mathematics in the morning. How are these initial assumptions reflected in classroom practice? Is time broken into further units with the emphasis upon particular parts of the mathematics curriculum and is this reflected in the lessons which are taught? It is to an examination of such issues that we now turn.

TIME AND THE MATHEMATICS CURRICULUM

The staff at Elm Park Primary had spent a large portion of their time during a NUPE strike organizing a mathematics syllabus and collecting together the material which related to particular themes and topics. Guidelines for the teaching of mathematics were also prepared and indicated the teachers' aims for pupils with regard to this subject. Both the syllabus and the 'NUPE sheets'[25] itemized aspects of mathematics to be covered within each year group. While there were some differences between the two documents they both introduced the work for each year by beginning with the teaching of number. Constant practice in the understanding of number was a feature of both the infant and junior classrooms as interviews which discussed the pattern of mathematics lessons revealed. One infant teacher outlined her lesson organization in the following way:

> Most of the lessons I start with little number rhymes and things like that so it is probably play for the first five minutes and we do all our little number rhymes. Then we probably do recognition of number – I'm not saying that we do it every day but at the beginning we do it every day. Then quick recognition of some shapes and then we go on to what concerns the Fletcher book for that particular day, or the section that we are working on. I am always going back. Each day you are revising something that you did either the day before or the week before, especially with these little ones. There is a similar daily pattern to the first year.

I was also able to identify very similar teaching patterns in infant classrooms in which I observed. Here again, the message transmitted to pupils is about what sort of mathematics is important; for example, recognition of number may be regarded as more important than work from the Fletcher books. The emphasis upon number work was also reflected in the junior classrooms. One teacher said:

> We do a lot of practice . . . [of number work] . . . when you are doing a lot of other things like area and capacity and lengths and directions and things like that, I still think that they need to keep their practice going in the computation. So therefore they do that as well – revision. Because otherwise they forget.

The teaching of mathematics, therefore, may influence children's attitudes towards the subject by the amount of time spent on teaching particular areas. Pupils might well assume that mathematics was really about performing well with numbers. It is also interesting to note that the infant teacher defined the beginning of her mathematics lessons as 'play' when the children were repeating number rhymes. This is a further division of time within the lesson. The use of pupils' time or the amount of time spent on a task has also been discussed by Galton and Willcocks[26] in relation to successful pupil learning. They explore the notion that teachers will be successful if they keep their pupils busy; a hypothesis which is strongly supported by some research[27]. Time on task, it is argued, will influence the amount of progress a pupil will make. However, Galton and Simon[28] found that intermittent workers often made as much progress as pupils who worked consistently and concluded that it was not the amount of time, but profitable use of time which was the important factor. Similarly, Charles Desforges and colleagues[29] describe how one pupil's attempt at a mathematical problem resulted only in confusion even though time was not wasted. They state[30]:

> repeating the old familiar advice to teachers about good management, increasing time on task, developing carefully structured schemes and the like is going to have the effect it always had: that is, no effect at all.

However, the results of such research do not appear to have permeated the primary classroom, where large amounts of time are devoted to the teaching of basic skills[31]. Certainly, Elm Park teachers devoted more time to the teaching of basic number work than to developing other mathematical concepts. Indeed, the way in which time was used during mathematics lessons which were not concerned with basic number work further supports the view that some tasks are only given the teacher's full attention if they are deemed worth spending time on, as an example of one fourth-year mathematics lesson I observed reveals. I recorded in my field notes:

> The lesson began with a reprimand from the teacher about writing on the desks after which the pupils were told to look at their *Beta Mathematics* books which were open at the section on circles. Mrs Pritchard, the class teacher, explained the difference between radius and radii and how the latter should be pronounced. This was followed by her saying that she felt they were all intelligent enough to do this work on their own and if they looked at the patterns on the top of the page they ought to be able to work this out for themselves. Carl Matthews had brought in some patterns of circles which were showed to the rest of the class – he had completed these at a previous school. Mrs Pritchard said that she believed his previous teacher

had shown him how to do these patterns – Carl agreed – Mrs Pritchard repeated that she thought here the children ought to be able to do them on their own.

The pupils were then asked to look at Question 3 and one child read the question out, which asked them to draw circles of different radii. The children were told how to measure the radius on their ruler using a compass and pencil and Mrs Pritchard demonstrated on the blackboard.

The children began their work in their books and Mrs Pritchard began to staple work to the classroom wall . . .

. . . In conversation at one end of the tables . . . one child confided: 'We're only doing this to have a rest from long division. After this we're going to do long division with decimals'. This remark was later verified by the teacher who said exactly the same thing.

This lesson was a complete contrast to earlier lessons I had observed on the teaching of long division, where the teachers' introduction was detailed and followed up by extra assistance for individual pupils during the lesson. If the content of a lesson is not worth all the teachers' time in introducing and monitoring the work in progress, what impression will pupils have? Does the conversation with Carl Matthews also illustrate that if pupils are 'intelligent enough' they do not need to use up a teacher's time by being taught? The hidden curriculum of this mathematics lesson was apparent to the pupils, as they recognized it as a rest activity before learning the 'real' mathematics of 'long division with decimals'. Both teachers and pupils use such time in a variety of ways, prioritizing their activities and allocating time accordingly. A major priority for staff at Elm Park was enabling pupils to retain work previously learned. The following section will examine how teachers included within their teaching programme time for remembering.

TIME FOR 'REMEMBERING'

The teaching of the mathematics curriculum at Elm Park can be seen to revolve around a number of features concerned with time. The problems that teachers encounter when trying to cope with the daily timetable, the different working speeds of pupils in mixed-ability classes and the demands of the school syllabus are also documented by Ball and others[32]. Another feature which influenced the teaching of mathematics at Elm Park was the teachers' belief that pupils were 'naturally' forgetful and, therefore, constant repetition was required. This first became apparent when the teachers discussed how they initiated work in mathematics at the beginning of an academic year. An infant teacher commented:

> Well, we usually start a little bit of revision to make sure that they know the numbers and revise sets and things like that.

The revision, therefore, concentrates upon the knowing of numbers and sets in this particular instance, while another infant teacher remarked:

> always start with some revisionary work – going back over what they have done the previous year.

A similar pattern for the beginning of the autumn term was reflected in some of the junior teachers' comments:

> I start with finding out what the children have achieved and where the problems start, usually with some computation work, to see where I need to go from there and then start working on the scheme – probably after the first week working through the Fletcher book and so on.

Here, the emphasis is upon revising 'computation work' combined with a diagnostic approach relating to pupil achievement and locating areas of difficulty. However, such revision periods were not only confined to the beginning of the year, they also occurred at regular intervals throughout the year as one junior teacher commented:

> Well, we go back all the time. Now last term, before Christmas, I taught them long multiplication. I went back to that two or three weeks ago and half of them had forgotten how to do it. I taught them long division after Christmas and if I go back to long division now I can guarantee two-thirds of them will have forgotten what to do.

> HB: So do you see that as an important process?

> Oh gosh yes! You can't expect them all to remember all the time, from one day to the next – some of them don't know what day it is.

So, alongside the yearly revision, there is also repetition of what is taught in previous terms. However, the reason given for such regular revision and repetition is that pupils 'forget'. The teacher also indicates that this is an ordinary characteristic of primary school pupils as she does not 'expect' them to remember. A very similar comment was made by another junior teacher who stated:

I think if you don't every so often throw in something that you have done before then it is gone and it is forgotten. Some children retain the germ of it . . .

Accordingly, time for remembering was quite an important feature of the mathematics curriculum for both infant and junior school pupils. This concept also reflects a part of the primary school teachers' ideology about children and the ways in which they learn. Here, 'forgetfulness' is natural and only to be 'expected' as far as the teacher is concerned. Indeed, the ideology of pupil 'forgetfulness' held major implications for the curriculum as it guided what the teachers taught and also shaped their future classroom practice. Such an ideology applied across the curriculum would mean an ongoing programme of repetition for the majority of pupils.

USE OF TEACHER AND PUPIL TIME

Time within a mathematics lesson may be used in ways not directly related to the teaching of mathematics. For example, time may be taken up with administrative matters or looking for items which are lost. While many such matters are relatively simple they can also have ramifications upon the curriculum and the use of both teacher and pupil time, as some notes from my field diary reveal concerning a lost pair of scissors.

9.30 a.m. – Gillian [Mrs Pritchard] explained that she had been away the afternoon before and, therefore, wanted to talk to the children about a missing pair of scissors. An assortment of maths questions were on the board which the children did while she sorted this out. She began by asking the children who had got the scissors out and put them away. They replied that it was Mrs Clay. Gillian sent a note to Mrs Clay. Meanwhile, one pupil got up to go to his maths group with Shirley [this teacher took small groups of pupils with special needs] and was told to wait. The note returned from Mrs Clay. Gillian told the children that Mrs Clay had not put the scissors away in the box according to her note and therefore demanded to know who was responsible. A girl from the back of the class went out to explain that she had put them in the box and was told that she would have to spend her playtime looking for them.

9.45 a.m. – Gillian began the mental arithmetic test . . . part way through Shirley came in asking for her group. Gillian replied that she would send them along in five minutes . . .

10.15 a.m. – . . . the children who go to Shirley were sent along.

This example of 'the lost pair of scissors' contains several interesting features relating to the use of pupil time. Indeed, the incident dominated the entire lesson, disturbing the usual class routine and resulting in the time a group of pupils should have spent working with a part-time teacher being cut to less than one-third. Time was also used for sending a note to Mrs Clay and waiting for a reply. The lost pair of scissors, therefore, involved the time of three teachers and a whole class of pupils and without a satisfactory conclusion to the matter being reached. However, once the discussion about the scissors ended at 9.45 a.m. the lesson began as it was intended to at 9.30 a.m. with a mental arithmetic test. The result was that work allocated for one hour had to be fitted into forty-five minutes.

The use of time in lessons for children who worked either quickly or very slowly was also evident in the mathematics teaching at Elm Park. As Delamont and Galton[33] suggest, pupils who work faster than their peers have to be kept occupied when they are finished or provided with more demanding tasks. It is also argued by Bennett *et al.*[34] that the main body of pupils within a class are provided with work which is too easy so that the slower ones may keep up more easily. The teachers at Elm Park spent quite a large portion of their time assisting pupils with difficulties while the rest of the class worked on the set task. Very often, this took the form of repeating or going over the explanation for the lesson, as an infant teacher commented:

> We have usually got a maths timetable for the morning. They do it in their books and I go through it. If anyone is having difficulty I go through it individually with them in the afternoon while the others are doing activities – it is the only thing you can do really. You have usually got a few and that is why we keep the activities more or less for that. And for any who have been away of course which is another problem. So it is usually individual work in the afternoon.

Here, the teacher discusses how she assists pupils individually with their mathematics in both the morning and the afternoon. A practice which will further reinforce the hidden curriculum of mathematics being viewed by pupils as a high-status subject and one in which, therefore, it is important to achieve success. Similarly, pupils who have been absent from school are also regarded as 'a problem' by teachers, who think that they need individual work in the afternoon apart from the 'activities' provided. Indeed, this teacher regarded the afternoon time as being specifically set aside for this purpose, as she said 'we keep the activities more or less for that'. It would appear, then, that if pupils are unable to do their mathematics in the morning they are given more practice in the afternoon. Such 'assistance' from teachers might be interpreted as 'punishment' by pupils.

Time to assist pupils individually was also perceived as a problem by other Elm Park teachers, some of whom saw class management and 'discipline' as important factors in the use of pupil time. One junior teacher said:

> There are lots of different forms of discipline and I think discipline of behaviour, discipline of a set procedure, routine, is the first of those disciplines on the way to learning. I don't think that without it you are going to learn much. It is all very easy for kids to wander around and look very busy and be doing absolutely nothing but if they are slotted and told what to do, when to do it and how to do it there is a very easy way then of checking on how much they have done.

The discipline of 'routine' and having 'set procedures' is, therefore, important for the quality of pupil learning according to this teacher. If children 'look busy' and 'wander around' they are not considered to be using their time usefully. Here, the proper use of pupil time during lessons is equated with being 'told what to do, when to do it and how to do it' and therefore supports an input–output model of pupil learning. This view was also reflected in another interview with a junior teacher, who was discussing how she went about helping children who have difficulty with mathematics. She said:

> It's like these two little tots down here. I sit with them and I do it with them, whereas the others now they know what they are doing, get them trained that we do this and we do that . . .

The emphasis here is upon 'training' pupils to know what to do. It appears that this in fact is a necessary strategy to enable the teacher to spend time with individuals.

Not all Elm Park teachers, however, simply repeated work for their pupils; a diagnosis of the pupils' problem and a record of pupil progress was kept for the next teacher, according to a third junior teacher:

> Well, I just keep working with them, probably in the dinner hour or something. Giving them extra work. Some concepts they are not

ready to take anyway. So I would make a note of the fact that they hadn't got a concept and it would go on the record at the end of the year for the next teacher.

The status of mathematics as a major curriculum subject is reinforced through having to work at the subject during the dinner hour. In this instance, pupil time outside lesson time is encroached upon in the case of children who find mathematics difficult.

The above examples illustrate how teachers use their own time and organize pupil time partly in relation to their beliefs about the ways in which pupils learn. Most teachers at Elm Park made use of some practical apparatus in some of their lessons. However, only one teacher considered that mathematics was a subject which could be regarded as fun:

> . . . I like to see the children achieve something. I like to try and avoid that anxiety thing I had as a child. I think maths is where you can have games and can make it fun . . .

This particular viewpoint is based upon this teacher's personal experiences of learning when young. She stresses the importance of enjoying a subject in order to be able to achieve success. A slightly different view was expressed by other teachers which was related to the amount of time available for the teaching of mathematics. For example, one teacher I asked about using 'maths games' replied:

> I just don't have time. By the time we've finished our lesson and we've done our – I suppose I could use them in other lessons or when they have finished what they are doing, I just don't get them [maths games] up here.

The importance of using time for 'work' rather than 'games' was also evident in the infant school even though the Fletcher mathematics scheme (*Mathematics for Schools*) indicated by a signal at the top of a page where a particular game might be appropriate. One infant teacher described how she used the Fletcher books with pupils:

> I always say 'look at the instructions at the top'. We always read that through together before they start. Never really take much notice of that really – I don't know if they [the pupils] do or not – but we always read the top part and go through it.

HB: They have little games signals as well somewhere don't they, in different places?

IT: The pages with the games on?

HB: [pointing in the Fletcher book] That sort of thing.

IT: Yes, to be quite honest we often don't get around to those . . .

Such activities, therefore, are not considered important by this teacher for the mathematical development of pupils and even when the use of games is suggested within the mathematics scheme, it is often ignored.

Where mathematical games were used with pupils they were only to be played with when the 'work' was finished. As one teacher explained:

> . . . we have got a fairly large number of maths games available in the school and last term I brought a lot of these up into the class-room. When children have finished their maths work they can come and get these games and play with them in their place. These will reinforce various mathematical concepts and be fun for them and they were very popular with the children. It did not lead to rushing their maths so they could get at the games because I would usually check just roughly anyway that they had got most of their sums right, or all their sums right, before they could go on to their maths games . . .

Time allocated for 'work', therefore, is concerned in this instance, with getting 'sums right' and only when this hurdle has been successfully negotiated may pupils spend their time on other activities. Use of time in primary classrooms is clearly divided, therefore, into high-status and low-status activities, and encourages pupils to believe that academic work such as mathematics is more worthwhile than many other skills taught in schools, such as practical and creative activities.

CONCLUSION

This chapter has illustrated how time is a highly significant factor in the teaching of the primary curriculum. Some basic areas of the curriculum, such as mathematics, are allocated a large proportion of pupil time each day, while other curricular activities such as science, history, geography and art may only appear on the timetable once or twice a week. At Elm Park Primary the amount of time spent on the teaching of mathematics held implications for the hidden curriculum, as this would suggest to pupils that mathematics was a higher-status subject than other less frequently taught subjects. This was reinforced in a number of ways;

for example, the division of time within the lesson where 'work' was regarded as completing 'sums'; or the repetition of work and use of pupil time during the dinner hour or the afternoon session. Time spent in such a way would indicate to pupils that they had to be successful in mathematics and that it was an important subject.

Time within the primary school is very precious for both teachers and pupils. Indeed, teachers may complain that they do not have sufficient time for staff meetings and work in curriculum development. One junior teacher was particularly clear on this point:

> . . . there is very little time in school for teachers to get together. There just is no time. None at all in primary school.

Use of time, therefore, is especially important. The way in which time is allocated to subjects or areas of learning may influence the balance and range of the curriculum which is taught. For some pupils at Elm Park, mathematics in the morning may have been followed by more mathematics in the afternoon.

This example of the teaching of a mathematics curriculum may hold implications for the primary curriculum as a whole. As the research at Elm Park revealed, mathematics teaching was given tremendous curricular emphasis. Accordingly, if such emphasis is placed upon the teaching of other subjects regarded as 'basics' such as reading and writing, little time will be left over to devote to a broader curriculum.

The quality of pupil learning and the ways in which children learn are cross-curricular concerns. Elm Park teachers generally allocated the morning for the teaching of mathematics while the afternoon was used for a variety of activities. Such an allocation of time not only makes assumptions about children's cognitive processes but also relegates the 'non-basic' curriculum to the least favourable times of day, according to primary school teachers, for optimum learning. The quality of pupil learning, therefore, across a range of activities may be affected by the amount of teaching time allocated to certain subjects and their consequent regard by teachers and pupils as a high-status activity.

Teacher ideology concerning the ways in which pupils learn is a significant factor where curriculum planning and development are concerned. The case study of Elm Park revealed that many teachers considered their pupils to be forgetful and planned their annual and weekly mathematics timetables accordingly. Many teachers began the academic year with some form of revision or testing in basic number work such as addition, subtraction, multiplication and division. This pattern of repetition or 'going over' work which had been previously taught was considered an essential part of the curriculum. 'Forgetting' work which had been taught a term earlier was considered natural for primary school pupils and, therefore, time had to be built into the teaching programme to accommodate this.

What teachers do, therefore, in both curriculum planning and practice is closely linked to their ideologies about the ways in which pupils learn, and their understanding of pupils' ability to retain knowledge. Each teacher at Elm Park used his or her time in the way that they considered the most effective and appeared to try to maximize learning by increasing the amount of time spent on mathematics. However, this 'mastery learning' approach to teaching has been criticized[35] and it has been argued that the amount of time spent on a task will not necessarily improve the quality of pupil learning. Greater 'match' between pupil ability and curriculum content across the range of curricular activities is advocated by HMI and other educationalists. However, while time on task continues to be seen by teachers as a major way of improving the quality of pupil learning experiences, the development of a broadly based curriculum in the primary school where the humanities, arts and sciences have equal status, is unlikely to be achieved. Similarly, the division of amounts of time to be spent on core and foundation subjects in the national curriculum provides another dimension to the use of time within the primary school and will bring with it new implications for what teachers and pupils do in primary classrooms.

REFERENCES AND NOTES

(1)   Education, Science and Arts Committee. *Achievement in Primary Schools*, Vol. I. London: HMSO, 1986.
(2)   *See* Board of Education. *Report of the Consultative Committee on the Primary School* (the Hadow report). London: HMSO and CACE, 1931, and DES. *Children and Their Primary Schools* (the Plowden report). London: HMSO, 1967.
(3)   *See* DES. *Mathematics for Ages 5–16* (Proposals of the Secretary of State for Education and Science and the Secretary of State for

Wales). London: DES/WO, 1988; DES. *Science for Ages 5–16* (Proposals of the Secretary of State for Education and Science and the Secretary of State for Wales). London: DES/WO, 1988.

(4) DES. *The Curriculum from 5–16*, Curriculum Matters 2, HMI Series. London: HMSO, 1985.

(5) Ibid., Curriculum Matters 17, p. 9.

(6) Ibid., Curriculum Matters 13, p. 7.

(7) Ibid., Curriculum Matters 16, p. 7.

(8) Alexander, R. J. *Primary Teaching.* London: Holt, Rinehart & Winston, 1984, p. 48.

(9) Simon, B. 'The primary school revolution: myth or reality?'. In Simon, B. and Willcocks, J. *Research and Practice in the Primary Classroom.* London: Routledge & Kegan Paul, 1981, pp. 7–25.

(10) *See* Bennett, N. *Teaching Styles and Pupil Progress.* Wells, UK: Open Books, 1976; Galton, M. J., Simon, B. and Croll, P. *Inside the Primary Classroom.* London: Routledge & Kegan Paul, 1980.

(11) Campbell, R. J. *Developing the Primary School Curriculum.* London: Holt, Rinehart & Winston, 1985.

(12) Pollard, A. *The Social World of the Primary School.* London: Holt, Rinehart & Winston, 1985.

(13) DES. *Primary Education in England* (survey by HMI). London: HMSO, 1978.

(14) Harlen, W. 'The role of assessment in "matching" '. *Primary Education Review*, **13**, 6–8, 1982.

(15) *See* King, R. *All Things Bright and Beautiful? A Sociological Study of Infants' Classrooms.* London: Wiley, 1978, pp. 16–23.

(16) *See* Sharp, R. and Green, A. *Education and Social Control: A Study in Progressive Primary Education.* London: Routledge & Kegan Paul, 1975; King, R., op. cit.; Pollard, A., op. cit.; Burgess, H. *The Primary Curriculum and Classroom Practice.* London: Allen & Unwin, forthcoming.

(17) The name of the school and all teachers' names referred to in this chapter are pseudonyms in order to protect confidentiality.

(18) Delamont, S. and Galton, M. J. *Inside the Secondary Classroom.* London: Routledge & Kegan Paul, 1986.

(19) King, R. op. cit., pp. 18–19.

(20) Education, Science and Arts Committee, op. cit., p. xci 6.31.

(21) Education, Science and Arts Committee, op. cit., p. xci 6.32.

(22) DES, 1985, op. cit.

(23) Hargreaves, D. H., Hestor, S. K., and Mellor, F. J. *Deviance in Classrooms.* London: Routledge & Kegan Paul, 1975.

(24) Pollard, op. cit., p. 161.

(25) These sheets were named 'NUPE' as they were prepared during a strike of members of the National Union of Public Employees. They were for use with the scheme *Mathematics for Schools* and itemized which sections of mathematical texts and other materials in Elm Park were relevant for the teaching of a variety of mathematical topics.

(26)   Galton, M. J. and Willcocks, J. *Moving from the Primary Class-room*. London: Routledge & Kegan Paul, 1983.

(27)   *See for example* Harnischfeger, A. and Wiley, D. 'Conceptual issues in models of school learning'. *Journal of Curriculum Studies*, **10** (3), 215–31, 1978.

(28)   Galton, M. J. and Simon, B. *Progress and Performance in the Primary Classroom*. London: Routledge & Kegan Paul, 1980.

(29)   Desforges, C., Bennett, N., Cockburn, A. and Wilkinson, B. 'Understanding the quality of pupil learning experiences'. In Entwistle, N. (ed.) *New Directions in Educational Psychology. 1. Learning and Teaching*. Basingstoke, Hampshire: Falmer Press, 1985, pp. 161–172.

(30)   Ibid., p. 166.

(31)   DES, 1978, op. cit.

(32)   Ball, S., Hull, R., Skelton, M. and Tudor, R. 'The tyranny of the "devils mill" '. In Delamont, S. *Readings on Interaction in the Classroom*. London: Methuen, 1984, pp. 41–57.

(33)   Delamont, S. and Galton, M. J., op. cit.

(34)   Bennett, N., Desforges, C., Cockburn, A. and Wilkinson, B. *The Quality of Pupil Learning Experiences*. Hove, East Sussex: Lawrence Erlbaum Associates, 1984.

(35)   Galton, M. and Willcocks, J., op. cit.

Chapter 3

Class Teaching and Curriculum Support

Norman Thomas

EDITOR'S COMMENT

One of the essential characteristics of the primary school is the autonomy of the classteacher in the classroom. This creates a distinct impression; of varied activities, lively displays, of reading corners and collections of materials, all giving a visual equivalent to the complexities of learning. It also draws attention to the varied abilities of the teacher. She demonstrates expertise in all aspects of the curriculum, from the physical to the aesthetic. But she is also perceived as a social and emotional centre. The role of the classteacher is one where expertise lies in understanding children as individuals, rather than in the purveying of knowledge.

It could be argued that the classteacher emerged as a model because of the small size of so many primary schools. There are still comparatively few schools which could employ enough staff to provide for specialists in all curriculum areas and although there are moves to concentrate resources on larger schools, this will not diminish the continuing need for generalist teachers.

But to some extent every teacher, however much she ostensibly specializes in one area of the curriculum, is expected to know a great deal about many subjects. Not only is it crucial to understand the children's process of learning in relation to the curriculum, but it is crucial to apply new knowledge to every part of the curriculum. Every teacher is expected, and is cajoled by the government and advisers, to know about information technology, the world of industry, health education and multicultural education, and to build these into her teaching. We are, in fact, creating new kinds of generalist.

We can always detect a tension between the generalist teacher, whose specialism is knowing about individual children's patterns of learning, and the subject specialist. But as the following chapter makes clear, the dichotomy is by no means so simple. Just as with the terms 'formal' and 'informal' to describe different approaches to teaching, what seems at first to be a plausible simplification can, on close analysis, turn out to obscure the real issues. The important distinctions between styles often lie in the acute perception of the children, rather than in the performance of the teacher. It is the children, in the end, who are the analysts of the teacher's role, who perceive the relationship between subject knowledge and its delivery, just as they know what real formality or informality mean.

Debates about curriculum expertise do not always take into account the relationship between one subject and another, as seen in the uses made of topic work. One of the opportunities for primary teachers, after all, is integration, seeing the crucial relationships that are formed between separate areas of study. Teachers, after all, need to vary their styles of teaching, and this automatically implies making use of different areas of the curriculum.

Underlying the question of the role of the teacher is the question of class size; but even this is far more complex an issue than it might appear to those of us who feel constantly overloaded and who feel that even one or two fewer in the classroom (especially *those* two) would make all the difference. In all the research reports about class size the conclusion is that class size does not have a simple relationship to children's achievement[1]. As the following chapter makes clear, decisions about the best use of resources must involve many classroom factors. This is why its stress on planning is so important. ■   (C.C.)

There are two major beliefs held by many concerned with primary education. The first is that the individual characteristics of each child should be taken into account in what is done in schools; the second is a belief in the system in which each class is the responsibility of one teacher, i.e. the class:teacher system. They predate even the Hadow report on primary schools[2]. This chapter is principally concerned with the second belief, but it also has implications for the first, and it might be as well to begin by reaffirming the importance of taking a child's current abilities, interests and aptitudes into account when deciding what direction his learning should take. The word 'deciding' in the last sentence includes the possibility, even the pleasure, of concluding that the child should do what he has chosen, unmodified by debate.

BREACHES IN THE CLASS:TEACHER SYSTEM

The class:teacher system has a long history but it has been breached for a number of reasons over the years. The breaches have been of several kinds. A small proportion of children have needed closer attention of a teacher than can be given to the whole class and so has been taught by an additional teacher who can concentrate on their needs: the children may, for example, have found learning to read difficult or, more commonly recently[3] than formerly, be thought to require special stimulation because they learn quickly. Sometimes, but by no means always, the teacher has been specially trained or at least self-trained to diagnose and treat these characteristics of children. In other work with individuals, small groups or classes, the teacher's special expertise has been paramount, for instance competence in playing a musical instrument (a violin or a clarinet, a piano or a guitar) that a child is learning to play or that is considered a necessary accompaniment to children's singing. Less now than during a brief period in the late 1960s – despite the growing number of children whose home language is not English – the expertise is in speaking a foreign language so that children may become proficient in it. In other circumstances an eager or compassionate teacher has stood in for an infirm colleague no longer fit to take physical education; an extension of this has led some teachers but not others to play the leading part in training school teams in summer or winter sports, in principle not unlike the enhancement groups arranged for academically gifted children.

Usually in larger schools, but sometimes in smaller, children in two or three classes may be rearranged with the object of making the children within a group more homogeneous in some aspect. The most common practice has been to separate boys and girls for games or for certain kinds of craft; this practice, certainly for the second purpose, has diminished and should have disappeared before now. On the other hand there has been some increase in setting: the regrouping of children for one or more subjects so as to make teaching groups of children who are more similar in their levels of attainment[4].

Perhaps it should not have come as a surprise that HMI found in their 1978 survey of primary schools[5] that 25 per cent of classes with 7-year-olds[6] and 46 per cent of classes with 11-year-olds were taught by a teacher other than the classteacher for between two and five hours each week, and smaller proportions for even longer. Of the classes with 7-year-olds, 73 per cent used at least one teacher other than the classteacher and for the 11-year-olds the figure was 90 per cent. Of the classes of older children, 43 per cent each used three or more teachers.

The causes of breaches in the class:teacher system can be summarized as follows: some children need especially to be taught individually or in groups smaller than the whole class; the children as a whole are (or at least are thought to be) too disparate for the work to be done in a part of the curriculum and classes must be rearranged; a class teacher is unable to teach a necessary part of the curriculum and another must be brought in; or a teacher's enthusiasm or special skill is judged worth using. A number of these factors may apply at once.

Before concluding that the class:teacher system is a myth, it is as well to consider the figures in the HMI survey obversely. Assuming the school week to be 25 hours long, 83 per cent of classes with 11 year olds were taught by one teacher for at least 20 hours each week, and the corresponding figure for classes with 7 year olds was 96 per cent. It was certainly true in 1976, and it is probably about as true today, to say that by far the greatest part of the teaching a primary school child receives is by his classteacher, but that the system is not as pure as is sometimes supposed.

SPECIALIZATION IN SECONDARY SCHOOLS

The situation is very different in secondary schools, and 11 year olds taught mainly by their classteacher in July may meet ten teachers a week in the following September; though a significant proportion of secondary schools have worked to make the number smaller. It can hardly be the case that the children alter during the intervening summer holiday as dramatically as that change suggests, and one is left to suppose that the differences are in the nature of the schools. In the secondary schools the argument for providing many teachers is that each must be as competent as possible in the subject she teaches. The case for subject specialization becomes stronger as the children get older and more knowledgeable and is probably quite irresistible for the great majority of 15-year-olds. The provision of specialist teaching for them makes more difficult the arrangement of generalist teaching for the younger children.

SOME ADVANTAGES AND STRAINS OF THE CLASS:TEACHER SYSTEM

Why should primary schools hold to the class:teacher system? Do they, in part, do so because it is particularly advantageous to the younger children, and because arranging a class:teacher system for them makes it more difficult to arrange specialist teaching for the older children? One consequence of widespread specialist teaching is that schools adopting the practice must be more generously staffed than those where each teacher has her own class, except when swapping on a one-to-one basis. Not, it will be noticed, *should be*, but *must be*. They must because it is just about impossible to arrange a timetable allowing the interweaving of specialist staff unless there is some excess of the number of teachers over the number of classes or groups to be taught. Secondary schools have become better staffed than primary schools with little emphasis on their need to reduce the sizes of teaching groups – except in requiring smaller than average numbers for practical subjects – but with much emphasis on the need for specific teaching roles.

But no one reading through the evidence given to the Parliamentary Select Committee during its inquiry into primary education[7] could be in any doubt that it was on grounds of principle that its witnesses were firmly against specialist teaching in the full secondary school sense being adopted by primary schools. The arguments for the class:teacher system have been put more than once. Young children have a greater sense of security when they have one teacher. Teachers and children can get to know each other better because they are together for a longer time and because they engage in a wider variety of activities. The daily programme can be adapted more easily to changing circumstances where only one teacher's programme is involved. The programme of work can be more of a piece because the teacher knows what is being done in each part. A child's strengths as revealed in one part of the work can be used to overcome uncertainties and weaknesses in another.

The arguments are very persuasive within their limits, and who would argue against the principle that the organization of an institution should be as simple as will allow it to be effective? The arguments depend on assumptions. One is that the teacher takes advantage of the opportunities the system provides. Another is that the child and the teacher are in accord, not in conflict: if there is conflict it would be better to have a change of teacher or the day will seem endless to both. So far as these two caveats are concerned, it is probably safe to say that in the vast majority of cases the advantages are to the class:teacher system. Other caveats are not so easily dismissed and include factors that have led to the breaches described earlier. Those to do with the formation of small groups require little further comment, though it is worth noticing that small groups can be and are formed within a class with no demand for an additional teacher. What characterizes the groups that use an extra teacher is their need for teaching which is unusually well informed or is concentrated and relatively prolonged, say for thirty minutes at a stretch. It is possible that concentrated teaching should be given much more frequently, not only to children who are slow or quick but to all at points in their learning when such teaching would take them through to the next stage. Given the right staffing levels and a less rigid attitude towards the class:teacher system, much higher achievement might be possible and considerable benefits might accrue.

More thought needs to be given to caveats relating to the adequacy of a teacher's capacity in the various aspects of learning to be introduced to the children. Two obvious facets are apparent in the examples of the use of specialist teaching given earlier: the ability of a teacher to do physically what is necessary if the teaching is to be effective, mainly so as to provide a suitable model for the children; and the knowledge a teacher has of what a child should learn, including learning to do and learning about. A third, not quite so obvious in the examples used, is a teacher's knowledge of how best to teach the skill, idea or information involved, or develop a child's interest and aptitude: that is to say, the methodology to be employed.

The question is: can the typical primary school teacher, or anyone else for that matter, be expected to have the physical skills, adequate knowledge in the various parts of the curriculum, and sufficient knowledge of the methodologies available to cover the whole range of work of the children, youngest to oldest, in a primary school? Or are shortcomings limited to those for which teachers additional to classteachers are already called in?

CHANGES IN THE DEPTH AND RANGE OF THE CURRICULUM

The question can only be answered as a result of making some assumptions about the curriculum and about children's capacities for achievement. If the curriculum and the expectations of children now were as they existed in 1944, then the answer could only be in the affirmative. Primary school teachers were almost without exception either classteachers or heads or both. There was some specialization for music and perhaps for physical education, but the teachers who took these subjects with more than one class were commonly also classteachers. Not too much attention was given to what the non-specialist teacher did with the specialist's class; the matter was often arranged between the two teachers or settled for the sake of the school timetable, but frequently it was a case of doing something easily contained in the time available – poetry was a possible victim – and not too distasteful to the incomer. Where the specialist took many classes, say all eight for two periods a week each in music, the whole of the literature and a miscellany of other subjects for her class could be in the hands of a mixture of others, and with only minimal efforts at co-ordinating them.

But the curriculum is not as it was in 1944 and will change further in many schools with the introduction of the national curriculum. The argument is often put forward that it is now broader, and so it is. Despite some financial difficulties, music in schools introduces children to a wider range of instruments than formerly, and in schools that are good at music there may be an orchestra, various smaller instrumental groups, and children may be composing as well as playing instruments and singing. Despite the aspersions sometimes cast on efforts to get the children to absorb information, the range of matter they deal with is wider, and far more likely to include material about the locality: present and past industries, the kinds of people who lived and live in the neighbouring streets, and so on. Even if there were no other good reason, the dissemination of up-to-date accounts of life elsewhere through television makes it important that teachers help children to acquire accurate and balanced accounts of life in other parts of the world. The number of titles in the school collection of books is vastly greater than in 1944 when so many were in sets of forty, and new titles are published monthly. The topics in mathematics now include some that would have been unfamiliar to sixth-formers in 1944: sets, tesselation, matrices, some esoteric number series with names like Fibonacci. Religious education requires far more than the retelling of a fairly small number of stories from the Bible with an account or two of the life of a more recent Christian. Every child should be developing an understanding of what it means to live in a culturally and religiously diverse society. Taken together, schools now employ a wider range of materials in art and craft and are more than beginning to incorporate design and technology in the making of things that move as well as look good.

However, what may be a more important change than the amount of ground covered is the depth to which it is cultivated. Some of the implications for depth are easy enough to deduce from the preceding paragraph. Good examples are to be found in science, where there is some evidence in the later surveys of HMI[8] of an increase in observational and experimental science which calls on children to look carefully, to differentiate between superficially similar things, to form views about why things are as they seem, and to devise ways of testing hypotheses formed. The national curriculum will require further extensions. Even in parts of the primary school curriculum that have always been regarded as essential, such as teaching children to read, there have been changes of requirement. It is no accident that the Watts–Vernon and the NFER NS6 tests have been replaced for the purposes of national monitoring by more varied tests designed by the NFER under the auspices of the APU[9]. The earlier tests were series of sentences, gradually increasing in reading difficulty, from each of which a word was missing; children were asked to choose the correct word from a number of possibilities. The new tests require children, among other things, to read a short story and to show not only that they know the facts included but also the implications that may be drawn. The larger collections of books in schools has made it imperative that children acquire library skills, so that they learn how to look for a book and how to deal with it. Extended individual and group topic work cannot be done effectively unless children learn to use indexes and contents pages, and how to vary their reading styles according to whether they are skimming or studying closely. A substantial number ought, by age 11, to be accustomed to comparing two or more texts in order to search out similarities and differences, and to check upon them. The assessment procedures recommended by the Task Group in Assessment and Testing, accepted by the government, require the development of educationally valuable but still more sophisticated assessment arrangements[10].

The introduction of computers into primary schools might be thought of as an extension of the curriculum, and of course it is. But the opportunity given for the development of clear thinking is more important than training in the use of the keyboard – of whatever shape – or programming. The chance to take the physical drudgery out of re-drafting opens up considerable possibilities for editing that is concerned with the choice of words, with sentence order, with the quality of the argument, and goes far beyond, though includes, grammar and orthography and other conventions of writing. Data collection and arrangement through the computer make possible insights that are difficult to come by through more laborious forms of recording; and the use of a computer language like LOGO[11] gives children the chance to develop an economy and precision of thought concurrently with anticipating and testing out its implications.

CHANGES IN METHODOLOGY

The curriculum is expanding in both breadth and depth, and all the indications are that it will and must continue to do so as the national curriculum is developed to remain in contact with what is going on outside schools and so be relevant to 'today's' children. Teachers and researchers also uncover more about the ways in which children learn and this should affect methods of teaching. Perhaps it is enough to pick three issues to stand for the rest. One relates to the teaching of reading. The Bullock report[12] was published in 1975 and is still regarded by many as significant in the teaching of English in schools. Although its index contains only two references to the use of context cues in reading, their use is considered in some detail in paragraphs 6.26 to 6.38 and the chapter includes a reference to the work of Frank Smith[13]. But the emphasis is less than would probably occur in a similar report today and, by comparison, there is extended discussion of the problem of matching the relatively few graphemes to the comparatively many phonemes. What proportion of the teachers of young children have been able to keep up-to-date with the discussion? How far should all primary school teachers be following the current shifts of view about the nature, place and teaching of a model of the English language?

The second issue also concerns language, but this time oral language, and it may have even more powerful consequences for a significant number of children. When the committee charged with identifying good practice in ILEA[14] primary schools was sitting, it early on became interested in the practices of some schools that seemed particularly effective in their work with children who had little or no English when they first came to school. They used, and sometimes swore by, practices that were different in detail. What they shared was the capacity to show their pupils beyond doubt that the teachers respected the children's home languages and a determination to enable them to acquire English not because it was superior to the language with which they were more familiar but because it is a liberating acquisition for anyone living in England. It seems such a simple idea as hardly to merit mentioning: unless one also applies it to non-standard dialects of English. The idea that standard English should be offered as a useful alternative rather than a correction of Cockney or Creole or North Tyneside is rarely practised. Yet the notion is well-supported theoretically[15] and if the shift from correction to augmentation could be made there is a good chance that the disadvantages that some dialect speakers suffer in the education system would be lessened.

These two examples are concerned with developing children's powers of language, but others might have been chosen covering almost every part of the curriculum. In 1981 the Cockcroft Committee[16] argued that mathematics teaching at all levels should include: exposition by the teacher; discussion between teacher and pupils and between pupils; appropriate practical work; consolidation and practice of fundamental skills and routines; problem solving; investigational work. Already one of its members, Hilary Shuard, has written[17] of the need for a significant shift in the practices used in teaching primary school children to allow for the fall in the importance of paper and pencil mathematics; what she has to say is an extension, not a retraction, of the Cockcroft proposals, just as more recent work on the teaching of reading has been an extension of the Bullock discussion.

THE NEED FOR SOME DIVISION OF RESPONSIBILITY

With such changes in the breadth, depth and methodology required if primary schools are to respond to the demands made of them and their pupils, is it reasonable to expect every teacher to keep abreast of what is going on and manage the curriculum unaided and virtually alone, except for the part traditionally played by teachers such as those specializing in music? The question is given more emphasis with the introduction of a statutory curriculum. The answer of the 1978 HMI survey of primary education was that the load had then become more than any one person could be expected to bear unaided and it drew attention to the much greater likelihood that children's work was better matched to their abilities where teachers with posts of responsibility had a marked influence on work throughout the school. For example[18], the more able 11-year-olds (as identified by their teachers) in the survey schools had their work well matched to them in two-thirds of the classes on which teachers with posts of responsibility had a strong influence. The same high degree of matching occurred in about one seventh of the classes where such teachers had little influence.

Both the Bullock and the Cockcroft reports proposed that primary schools should have at least one member of staff who took the lead in each of the aspects of the curriculum that were their concern. The former described the role as follows[19]:

> We prefer to think in terms of a gradual development from the class/teacher situation through co-operative working to a degree of specialism for the older children. In practice this would work as follows. Between the age of five and nine there would be a firmly based class–teacher relationship, but with a gradual extension of the involvement of other colleagues. There would be some need from a fairly early stage for the class teacher to refer to a colleague for more specialist help, but at this stage such help should be looked upon as supportive; that is to say, it would depend upon the occasion and the needs of the individual children.

The report goes on to say that the development towards specialist teaching would increase as children approached 13 years of age. Since English permeates the timetable it was thought not to follow that English should be taught as a specialist subject in primary schools, though some use of the specialist would need to be timetabled. The report recognized that more teacher time is required for joint planning, the interchange of ideas and for 'the expertise of some teachers to help with the problems of others'. In a later paragraph[20] the point is made that a teacher's special responsibilities in a small school may have to be broader than in a large school.

The essential ingredients of later discussion on this topic are well contained in the report, though not as fully teased out as they now have been. The distinction has become sharper between the teaching of children by specialists, and teachers exchanging specialist advice. Neither the provision of specialist advice nor the arrangement of specialist teaching necessarily requires separating the curriculum into subjects each to be timetabled separately, though there are other arguments for increasing the distinction between subjects as the children learn more. Additional teacher time is necessary to allow the interaction of ideas and people to take place. Schools with few teachers have to behave differently from schools with many teachers, though not necessarily by taking on broader responsibilities.

THE IDEA OF COLLEGIALITY

Some of the ingredients mentioned are self-evident or so widely accepted as to require no further discussion here, and there is little to be gained from tracing the argument step by step as it has developed, though one stage is of particular importance. R. J. Campbell[21] expressed it most clearly in his reference to 'the "collegial" primary school, predicated on the two values of *teacher collaboration* and *subject expertise*'. The notion of collegiality comes far closer to what has more recently been argued than does an argument about generalist versus specialist teaching.

THE BASIS OF A CO-ORDINATOR'S ADVICE

One issue that needs taking further is: what is the source of the advice that one teacher should be giving another? The obvious answers are personal experience, visiting other schools, in-service courses, and reading reports of inquiries, research and other people's practice. But that is only half the story. The co-ordinator – to use the term preferred by the Select Committee[22] – should be giving advice that is relevant to the children, teachers and conditions in the co-ordinator's own school. It is a long-standing principle of primary education that what is done with children should start from where they are. The principle applies more generally than to teaching children, and it is certainly of importance in advising teachers. Co-ordinators must know what is being done throughout their own school if they are to give appropriate advice.

THE FORMS IN WHICH A CO-ORDINATOR'S KNOWLEDGE MAY BE TRANSMITTED

There appears to be wide agreement that teachers acting as co-ordinators should pass on their knowledge during informal staff-room discussion; through leading formal staff discussion, sometimes after preparing draft papers and leading up to a written scheme of work or policy statement; and through showing in practice what can be done in their aspect of the curriculum.

Some witnesses to the Select Committee argued against the idea that co-ordinators should teach a class in the absence of the class teacher[23]. To do so, it was feared, would lead to the curriculum being fragmented. A combination of two things stand in the way of the absolute achievement of their goal. The first is the number of aspects of primary school work in which higher than average expertise is desirable from time to time. Taking witnesses to the Select Committee as the source, all concerned with particular fields of work except those involved with microcomputers argued for the presence of a co-ordinator to represent their interest. The second is: if a co-ordinator is to have time to get to know what is going on in other classes, let alone also teach children in them from time to time, and children are not to be taught other than in the presence of their class teacher, then the co-ordinator must have no responsibility for a class – for what, otherwise, would be happening to the co-ordinator's class while absent on co-ordinating duties? But it is outside the bounds of possibility and probably undesirable that primary schools should be staffed by a general teacher for each class and an equal or even greater number of specialists moving round from class to class. In fact, the notion of children being taught only in the presence of their classteacher is no longer a practical possibility, if ever it was. Absence through illness and attendance at courses has always produced changes of teacher. The proper and increasing insistence that primary school teachers should have 'non-contact' time will inevitably lead to more such occasions.

The question today is not whether classes should or should not be taught in the absence of their classteacher, but how such teaching can be kept to what is necessary to the enhancement of the children's learning. Too much interchange will at best fragment their work and at worst fritter time away. Too little diminishes the quality of what can be offered to them. The quality of what is done in the class of the teacher acting as a co-ordinator is as important as the quality of the work being done by the co-ordinator.

THE ENHANCEMENT OF THE CLASSTEACHER'S ROLE

There is no certain way of securing the coherence of the curriculum and the most effective use of time, but the best chance lies in enhancing the role of the class teacher *per se*. Bluntly: the classteacher should have responsibility for co-ordinating all the teaching of her class, no matter who is responsible for the time being, and for making sure that the incomer's time is used to best effect. That requirement should apply just as much in the case of the children having special help because they are slow at learning to read as to the case where the class is being taken for part of a session each week for half a term to stimulate their interest and knowledge of the local environment. The object is to ensure that the children perceive the curriculum as coherent, are alert to the connections between the various aspects of their learning, are aware that what is learnt in one connection may be useful in another. The place in which the learning occurs – whether it is in the classroom or elsewhere – and the presence of the classteacher can affect the ease with which the children's perceptions can be sharpened, but they are not the essence of the matter. Children who are easily distracted may sometimes best be taught separately from the class.

COMBINING THE CLASSTEACHER AND
CO-ORDINATING ROLES

The many facets of the work of primary schools that can be improved where there is an interested and informed teacher make it necessary to postulate that virtually all classteachers must also take on a co-ordinating role in compensation for no longer being expected, impossibly, to keep up with every aspect of primary school development. Many primary schools are too small to allow each teacher to be responsible for only one clearly defined aspect of the work. Even if the work is divided into the broadest of areas – say, aesthetic and physical education, language, mathematics, science, social education – five teachers are needed, and it is easily demonstrated that the broad headings cover hardly compatible elements. For example, aesthetic and physical education would have to cover music, drama, the plastic and graphic arts, dance, gymnastics, athletics, sports and probably design and technology as well; and who would be responsible for keeping in touch with the literature on assessing children's work and record keeping, or good practices in the promotion of health and safety in schools?

In small schools with only one, two or three teachers the load is too heavy even when divided broadly as the Bullock report suggests. There is a growing number of cases where teachers from three or four such schools share the task of keeping informed and act as co-ordinators across the cluster of schools. The implications of this are considerable. The appointment of a new teacher should no longer be thought to be the business of one school and its governors alone, for the balance of interests and skills of teachers in the group of schools ought to be taken into account when a vacant post is being filled. Not only do the teachers need time to get to know the work of their colleagues so that their advice is relevant, and access to the children when the classteacher is unable to proceed even with advice, they also need the means to travel. There are additionally good arguments for the children travelling for some purposes: for example to use resources that cannot be transported or to extend their social and geographical horizons. Clustering is not a cheap way of providing for children in small schools but it is a way of giving them something like equality of opportunity with children in larger schools so long as teachers in the larger schools are not expected, as sometimes happens now, to cope with unfairly larger teaching groups to pay for better provision in small schools.

THE NEED FOR ADDITIONAL TEACHING TIME

Whether the group of teachers working collegially is the staff of one school or a number of schools, the requirement for extra time remains. Sir Keith Joseph (now Lord Joseph), when Secretary of State, told[24] the Select Committee that he thought it necessary to provide 15 000 extra teachers for primary education to allow increased non-contact time presumably, among others, for the kinds of duties suggested here for co-ordinators. This number did not include any additional teachers necessary to deal with rising numbers of children, or to reduce class sizes.

It must be accepted that providing non-contact time, for whatever purpose, makes necessary larger registration classes than would be the case if every teacher was made responsible for a registration class. The Select Committee[25] concluded that it was wrong to suppose that primary school classes could safely be larger than secondary school classes; that the aim should be to reduce the sizes of registration classes with thirty or more pupils; but recognized that there might be circumstances in which a class of thirty to thirty-five could be justified. Fifteen thousand teachers is just about the equivalent of ten per cent of the primary teaching force in England, other than heads. To use them to reduce class size would, assuming the spaces could be found for the additional classes, lower the average sizes of registration classes by only two or three pupils. It is likely that far more benefit will accrue to both children and teachers if these extra numbers, assuming they are provided, are used to form much smaller teaching groups from time to time, to permit some time for preparation and in-service training in school hours, and the chance to share out expertise rather than expecting teachers to be masters of all subjects.

The time freed by this number of extra teachers is hardly excessive in terms of need, though it has to be accepted that the cost of provision is considerable. Their employment would almost certainly not achieve the 0.8 teacher contact time proposed by the National Association of Headteachers to the Select Committee[26]. (The present figure, including heads, is about 0.9.) The role of the additional teacher who has no responsibility for a registered class requires – for it already exists in some places – special protection in primary schools. When a teacher is away it is tempting to cancel the 'additional' teacher's programme. The advantages of the system will be seriously diminished if either heads or LEAs take this action, and of course nobody would dream of cancelling the programmes of secondary school teachers simply because they had no register to keep or because they were taking small groups for craft. The additional teacher's teaching programme should be as heavy and as sacrosanct as other teachers', neither more nor less. The role of the additional teacher should be to act as a co-ordinator in one or a group of aspects of the school's work, just like any other teacher. Through teaching classes or smaller groups, she should allow flexibility in the programmes of the other members of staff, including a knock-on effect by which a third teacher is helped, so extending interchange beyond the simple swapping of classes in the traditional music specialist style.

The organization of a school working collegially is more complex than that of a traditional primary school in which each teacher and class can be regarded separately and distinctly and is more complex and unpredictable day to day than the traditional secondary school with its pre-set timetabling of teachers and children. It can only be successful if the organizational arrangements are tied closely to the teaching requirements of the children. It would be a mistake to allow the organization to be more complex than it must be for the purposes it has to serve. The issues are: what are the children learning; what help do they need; who can provide it? If the classteacher can provide the teaching, if necessary with advice and help from a colleague acting as a co-ordinator, then so be it. If the classteacher cannot, then the co-ordinator must do the teaching. The arrangements may need to serve one child, a small group or the class as a whole. They may require one intervention by the co-ordinator or many. The potential advantages have to be set against the potential disadvantages, for example to the co-ordinator's own class, before deciding what to do in a particular instance.

CO-ORDINATING THE CO-ORDINATORS

This is not the place to discuss at length the notion of a school development plan, as proposed in *Improving Primary Schools*[27] and the Select Committee Report[28]. It is necessary to draw attention to the concept because the division of labour between primary school teachers described in this chapter could lead to a fragmentation of the school as well as the class curriculum if each co-ordinator is encouraged simply to look at what is done from her own viewpoint. If coherence is to be achieved in the school curriculum as a whole the various interests need to be brought into a common focus. The production of a school development plan to which each co-ordinator should contribute and from which each should draw can provide such a focus, and is a proper corollary to the introduction of a collegial system.

REFERENCES AND NOTES

(1)   King, N. *The Effects of Class Size*. Research Report Series No. 1. Towson, MA, USA: Lida Lee Tall Learning Resources Centre, 1988.

(2)   Board of Education. *Report of the Consultative Committee on the Primary School* (the Hadow report). London: HMSO and CACE, 1931.

(3)   National Foundation for Educational Research (NFER). Evidence given to House of Commons Education, Science and Arts Committee, Session 1984–85. London: HMSO, 1985, p. 349.

(4)   Ibid.

(5)   DES. *Primary Education in England* (survey by HMI). London: HMSO, 1978.

(6)   It should be noted that these 7-year-olds would be the oldest class of infants in a school arranging its classes strictly by school-year of birth.

(7)   Education, Science and Arts Committee. *Achievement in Primary Schools*, Vol. I. London: HMSO, 1986.

(8)   HMI. *Education 5 to 9*. London: HMSO, 1982, para. 4.10.

(9)   The Assessment of Performance Unit (APU) of the Department of Education and Science, set up in 1975 to 'promote the development of methods of assessing and monitoring the achievement of children at school, and to seek to identify the incidence of under-achievement'.

(10)   DES. *Task Group on Assessment and Testing: A Report*. By P. J. Black *et al*. London: HMSO, 1988.

(11)   Papert, S. *Mindstorms*. Brighton, UK: The Harvester Press, 1980.

(12)   DES. *A Language for Life* (Bullock report). London: HMSO, 1975.

(13)   Smith, F., *Understanding Reading*. NY, USA: Holt, Rinehart & Winston, 1971.

(14) ILEA (Thomas report). *Improving Primary Schools.* London: ILEA, 1985.

(15) Trudgill, P. *Accent, Dialect and the School.* London: Edward Arnold, 1975.

(16) DES. *Mathematics Counts* (Cockcroft report). London: HMSO, 1982.

(17) Shuard, H. *Primary Mathematics Today and Tomorrow.* London: Longmans/SCDC, 1986.

(18) Cockcroft report, op. cit., p. 106.

(19) Bullock report, op. cit., para. 13.13.

(20) Bullock report, op. cit. para. 13.23.

(21) Campbell, R. J. *Developing the Primary School Curriculum.* London: Holt, Rinehart & Winston, 1985, p. 152.

(22) Education, Science and Arts Committee, op. cit., para. 9.11.

(23) Education, Science and Arts Committee, op. cit., see references to para. 9.19.

(24) Evidence given to the Education, Science and Arts Committee, First Scrutiny Session, 26 November 1985, HC 86, Session 1985/6, Questions 54–55. London: HMSO.

(25) Education, Science and Arts Committee, op. cit., para. 14.85.

(26) Education, Science and Arts Committee, op. cit. para 9.50.

(27) ILEA Committee of Inquiry, op. cit., para. 3.93 ff.

(28) Education, Science and Arts Committee, op. cit., para. 13.13 ff.; HMI. *A New Teacher in School.* London: HMSO, 1982; op. cit., para. 14.156.

Chapter 4

The Teacher and Others in the Classroom

Gary Thomas

EDITOR'S COMMENT

It might have been deliberate, or it might have been, like so many consequences of legislation, an accident, but the national curriculum proposals meant that there would not only be increasing demands on teachers in terms of subject expertise, but on their ability to communicate that expertise. Both the sense of the all-rounder and the autonomy of the classteacher are eroded when teachers have to compare the performance of the children in their class against national criteria and with the performance of classes in other schools[1]. The work of children will be open to inspection and to comparison; the response to it will shift from celebration to justification.

But the classteacher was never as completely autonomous as might be implied. Such autonomy as she had has been steadily if undeliberately removed. Although open-plan schools were sometimes built to save money rather than for more philosophical reasons, they did cause groups of teachers to work more closely together, not only sharing resources and abilities, but allowing teachers to concentrate on particular interests and enthusiasms[2]. The development of curriculum statements and guidelines has necessitated not only discussion amongst colleagues, but, in a way that was first suggested by the Bullock report, the designation of a particular individual to co-ordinate the guidelines and to write them. All teachers find themselves needing to demonstrate what they are doing to parents. Classrooms are less and less private.

As this chapter shows, however, classrooms are already peopled by an increasing number of people playing a variety of roles, who not only hear what the teacher has to say about what she is doing, but who see her doing it. These colleagues, like student teachers, are there to help rather than criticize but there are few teachers who do not perceive a subtle difference between the exclusive relationship they engender with a class, and the awareness of someone else's presence in the classroom. They can be more self-conscious than the children.

Education is a co-operative process, and should be seen as such. Co-operation obviously helps children, whether it is between teachers and parents, or between different agencies concerned with children's welfare. This is seen most obviously in the case of children with special educational needs. It is hard to imagine how a teacher can survive without outside help and information. But an ability to organize a variety of contributions is yet another requirement of the experienced teacher.

With so many others in the classroom the teacher needs a new kind of professional expertise, not only in matching tasks to the individual needs of children, but also in matching people; not only being able to create a relationship with the children in the classroom but also with other adults. ■   (C.C.)

Much has been said and written about the involvement of parents in their children's schools. But it is not only parents who are moving into the classroom: a host of other people are entering classrooms to work alongside the classteacher. Most teachers will concur with the *spirit* behind these moves – whether they are to do with parental involvement or the integration of children with special needs. But they may become disillusioned when problems occur. And problems inevitably will occur (as the following case study demonstrates) if there is insufficient thought given to the idea. If we believe in the ideal of parental involvement, or integration, or community involvement, we need to find ways of making them work.

Case Study 1

Albert Street Primary School is a large primary school in Victorian buildings on the fringe of the inner part of a large northern city. The initial impression to the visitor is of greyness: the school is grey; the surroundings are grey, and the sky is (almost always) grey. The school has recently acquired a new headteacher after the last head retired after sixteen years at the school. Most of the staff who remain at the school were appointed around the same time as the original headteacher. The new head, Mr Joseph, is young, dynamic and full of ideas. He has something of a reputation amongst the staff as someone who will jump on any bandwagon. Mr Joseph has been recently been exploring the idea of increasing parental involvement in the school.

Mr Joseph has identified Miss Crosby, one of the two recently appointed members of staff at the school, as someone who will be receptive to the idea of parents working alongside her in the classroom. Miss Crosby completed her probationary year last year and currently takes a class of thirty-one first-year juniors. She has not heard very much about parental involvement but is willing to go along with the idea partly in response to Mr Joseph's enthusiasm. When the rest of the staff hear about the idea they are cynical about the reasons for it ('jumping on the parental involvement bandwagon'), cynical about its merits, and question the legitimacy of involving unpaid people in the classroom. There are murmurings about involving the Union. But no one is energetic enough to mobilize in opposition to the scheme, which goes ahead almost by default.

Miss Crosby is not confident in her dealings with parents and in response to Mr Joseph's suggestion she approaches two not very assertive parents to ask them if they would be willing to work alongside her in the classroom. Partly because they are not very assertive, they agree. Mrs Baker is an older parent of a family of five children, all of whom have passed through the school, and Christina, her youngest daughter, is now in Miss Crosby's class. Mrs Baker is a quiet person; she does some cleaning in the school on a part-time basis. Mrs Dunn is much younger than Mrs Baker and is the mother of Alan, also in Miss Crosby's class. She too is rather timid in her relationships with school. Both Alan and Christina are quiet, hard-working children though Alan is not progressing with reading as well as one might expect.

The parents are asked to visit the school on a rotating basis with Mrs Baker coming in on Monday and Wednesday mornings, and Mrs Dunn coming in on Tuesday and Friday. Neither Mr Joseph nor Miss Crosby has given either of the parents any very clear directions about what they are to do in the classroom, preferring 'flexibility', and allowing the parents to do what they think suits them best. So, each parent develops strategies for avoiding the strains which they immediately feel developing: each feels uncertain about what to do when the level of noise rises when Miss Crosby leaves the class; they feel uncertain about the 'new' maths, and about how to help children who come up to them for help with reading – do they sound out? Do they tell the children unfamiliar words? Mrs

Baker adopts the avoidance strategy of getting out of the children's way as much as possible, preferring to tidy books, mount work, etc. This is certainly helpful to Miss Crosby, although she is not fully aware of just how uncomfortable Mrs Baker is. Mrs Dunn adopts the strategy of becoming engrossed in helping any particular child whose work she feels happy supervising.

Miss Crosby sees clear deficiencies in the way that the 'parental involvement project' is operating, feeling that the parents are not really being involved in the life of the classroom. She can identify certain of the problems which are preventing better involvement but wonders just where to start in discussing this with the parents. In her uncertainty she does nothing at all. She is unwilling to ask Mr Joseph for help as he appears to have lost interest in the project and is now busy organizing a sponsored walk to collect for a video system for the school.

The rest of the staff are at best unwelcoming to the parents, who are not invited into the staff room at break and are relegated to standing and having their coffee in the small ante-room next door.

After two weeks Mrs Baker summons courage to explain to Miss Crosby that unfortunately she cannot come any more as she has obtained another part-time job. After a further week Mrs Dunn also withdraws.

Analysis of case study

Albert Street Primary is fictional (well, almost). But many will recognize the changes going on there and many will recognize the all too familiar picture of 'parental involvement' jumped on as the latest bandwagon with insufficient forethought or preparation. We need to look at some of the ways in which we can prepare for extra people in the classroom and avoid some of the problems which led to the demise of Albert Street School's initiative.

David Hargreaves[3] might once have been correct in saying that teachers think of teaching rather as they think of sexual activity – best done in private. But that no longer seems to be the case. Recently completed research shows that a quiet revolution has taken place in the primary classroom of the 1980s: people have moved into the primary classroom to such an extent that it is now the exception rather than the rule to find teachers who always work on their own[4].

To call this influx of people a revolution is no exaggeration: there are fundamental changes in the atmosphere of the class when other adults move into the territory of the teacher and her children. For other adults, many of them untrained or unpaid, or both, to move into this territory there has also been a revolution in our thinking on issues like professionalism. And there is a revolution in terms of opportunity: enormous gains can be achieved when parents are involved in hearing their children read at home, so how much greater may be the benefits if parents are participating at school, where the teacher's experience and advice are immediately available?

In my survey[4], 82 teachers in Oxfordshire completed timetables which showed how additional people had worked alongside them in a week. Parents had been participating in 87 per cent of the classrooms, and other adults had been involved in all but one of the classrooms. The range of activity of these extra people was enormous: parents were involved in hearing reading, taking groups for music, working on language and number, and many other activities. Peripatetic teachers would be doing highly specialized work with individuals or small groups of children with special needs. In total the range of activity covered by this heterogeneous group of participants is as great as that covered by the teacher.

The people who are moving into classrooms are from a variety of backgrounds with an enormous variety of expertise: they may previously have been associated with the special sector; they may be staff from peripatetic services; they may be ancillary helpers, or they may be parents. Alongside these 'prime movers' there are speech therapists, young people on YTS schemes, school governors, volunteers; all are moving into the new, open classrooms of the 1980s.

Such changes involve fundamental changes in the climate both of the classroom and the school. Major management implications follow. A host of problems and opportunities arise in thinking about the involvement of additional adults – whatever their background – in the classroom. The aim here is to explore some of those problems and opportunities by looking at some of the general implications of change.

As so many of the extra people who are moving into mainstream classrooms are moving there because of changes in thinking about special needs, especially since the Warnock report and the 1981 Education Act, I begin by discussing this area.

THE NEW PEOPLE IN CLASSROOMS – THE 'SPECIAL' PEOPLE

It is sometimes assumed that integration of children with special needs is taking place when children are merely occupying the same physical environment in a school. But often such 'integration' is only nominal and children's needs may be inadequately met. Worse than this, the very practices which are operated ostensibly to help these children, e.g. withdrawal, may in fact be stigmatizing them and thereby making it more difficult for them to learn. The effect of self-image upon ability to learn is well recognized. The conspicuous identification of those children who are to receive help through their removal from the room cannot foster positive feelings about the withdrawal or the activity associated with it. Children are not as easily stigmatized if additional help is provided *in* the classroom – as long as it is done with sensitivity.

Much thought has been given to the benefits of integration yet surprisingly little thought has gone into the means by which special sector staff will most effectively be deployed in ordinary school settings. Some of those people and the reasons for their moves are as follows.

Welfare assistants and ancillary helpers.   Statementing procedures under the 1981 Education Act have in some cases resulted in non-teaching assistance being allocated to meet the child's needs in the ordinary school setting. The amount that this occurs in practice varies a great deal depending on the nature of the child's problem and depending also on the policy of the funding Local Education Authority.

Peripatetic teachers.   Although there are small numbers of peripatetic teachers who are concerned with specialisms such as music, the largest body of these teachers is concerned with children who are experiencing reading difficulties. Peripatetic teachers also provide an invaluable service for children who have sensory disabilities. Increasingly, peripatetic teachers are seeing themselves working most effectively alongside the ordinary classroom teacher. The traditional model of the peripatetic teacher taking a small group of children for some special work away from the rest of the class is, in a post-Warnock era, becoming less tenable.

Nursery nurses.   Qualified nursery nurses form an indispensable ingredient in the effective operation of many special school classrooms. If they are employed to meet the needs of children in segregated settings then they should be employed to meet the needs of the same children in non-segregated settings.

Support services.   Speech therapists, physiotherapists and occupational therapists have all provided vitally important services for children with special needs and this has usually been provided in the special school setting or in a clinic. Recent trends will mean that such services will be needed more in the ordinary school setting. As time passes it is likely that larger numbers of imaginative schemes will be formulated for assimilating into ordinary classrooms the work of these professionals.

Remedial teachers.   In middle schools (and of course in secondary schools) teachers with responsibility for special needs have customarily withdrawn groups of children from their classes – and often therefore from the main curriculum of the school – for work on core areas of the curriculum. A different pattern is now emerging in some schools whereby staff from the remedial department are deploying their skills and resources throughout the main body of the school. Under such schemes remedial staff reach out to larger numbers of children and help those children without the stigma of withdrawal. They also more easily integrate their own work within the school's curriculum.

PARENTS IN CLASS

At the same time that special-sector staff are moving to the mainstream there is, for different but equally valid reasons, a move toward the increasing involvement of parents in their children's education. This is increasingly occurring at school in the classroom. While the domain of parents in the classroom has conventionally been needlework, cookery and craft, recent trends have seen parents helping in more formal areas of the curriculum, perhaps injecting enthusiasm about their own skills or expertise.

The involvement of parents in the education of their children has extended now beyond home-reading projects. There is now a widespread and radical reappraisal of the role of parents in the classroom. While controversy over the extent of such involvement still exists, it is probably true to say that the question is now more frequently *how* parents may best be involved in the classroom rather than *whether* they should be involved.

PROBLEMS AND OPPORTUNITIES

Whilst the classroom remained the domain of one person there was little need to explore, for example, teamwork, management of personnel, role relationships and the possible ways in which the teacher's job might most usefully be examined and differentiated. As the pattern of one person to one class becomes less common it becomes increasingly important that the problems and opportunities that are simultaneously created by these moves of additional people to the classroom are fully explored. The main aim of this section is to look at ways of maximizing the opportunities while minimizing the problems which may be associated with such changes.

Some of the possible problems may be categorized as follows.

Role ambiguity. As increasing numbers of people are involved in the execution of any task, the possibility for misunderstanding amongst them is magnified. With a highly complex task such as teaching, the potential for confusion about role definition is high when more than one person is present.

Diminishing returns. It has for a long time been realized that personal effectiveness may be reduced when tasks are shared[5]. People will unintentionally obstruct each other, or duplicate the other's effort. The extent to which this occurs depends greatly on the nature of the task and the number of people contributing. While many of the tasks which are being undertaken in the shared classroom would be carried out autonomously, thus reducing many of these effects, there are nevertheless bound to be certain problems to do with sharing the same physical space.

Confusion amongst children. There is the possibility that children may 'play off' one adult against another, thus diminishing the effectiveness and the credibility of each. Being used to having only one adult in the classroom, children may not fully understand how they should respond to the additional person or people. They may ascribe imaginary weightings to the importance of the various adults who are present and this may serve to accentuate distinctions which the classteacher would wish to minimize; it may on the other hand undermine the position of the teacher.

Any method of organizing the work of people within the classroom must take account of these negative consequences of having people sharing a task. But having dwelt on the *problems* which can arise from sharing a task it should be emphasized that effective teamwork can produce results which it would not have been possible for separate individuals – albeit working in the same physical space – to produce.

So how does effective teamwork take place without invoking all the problems to which I have just referred? A number of things may be done. We can aim to limit role ambiguity by specifying what each person will be doing; we can aim to reduce loss of effectiveness due to diminishing returns by establishing clear rules of working and identifying areas for work. We can also aim to make clear to the children in the class how the various adults will be operating.

But most important for effective teamwork in the classroom are differentiation and communication.

Differentiation. There are many competing demands on the teachers's time: it is often the case that in taking care of one aspect of her work, like giving a child individual teaching, the teacher may not be able to deal as adequately as she would like with other equally important and pressing matters. One of the main advantages which will accrue from the work of extra people in the classroom is that it will be possible to differentiate and thereby fulfil more easily the various activities which the teacher undertakes in the classroom.

Communication. There is no substitute in communication for having two (or more) people talking together in the same physical space. Notes and telephone messages are simply not as good – or worse, they may actually be counter-productive. Having those who are involved in children's education together in the same classroom aids communication wonderfully.

Although it *has* been possible in the traditional style of peripatetic teacher work to effect good communication between peripatetic teacher and classteacher, that style of work has not lent itself to such communication. Because the two teachers are working in physically separate environments, the opportunity for both formal and informal contact is limited. Such a position is aggravated by the peripatetic teacher's hectic work life. She will often be hurriedly 'packing up shop' to move to her next school. Clearly in this circumstance the chances of a meaningful dialogue are reduced. Moving into the classroom will not alleviate these problems but it will at least ensure the opportunity for each teacher to have immediate contact with the work of the other.

It must also be said that the great divide between school and home has meant that the aims of school have not always been clear or even apparent to parents. Nor have the concerns of parents always been accorded the respect which they deserve in schools. The presence of more parents actually *in* classrooms can only improve communication.

FACTORS TO BE CONSIDERED IN THE ORGANIZATION OF ADULTS IN CLASSROOMS

A central focus of this chapter is on the *organization* of extra people in the classroom. We must take it as given that these 'extras' are there. The arguments for or against their presence are well rehearsed and I do not propose to repeat them here. It seems to me that teachers, parents, volunteers and other professionals have now overcome the barriers to involvement; we are now confronting the problems and opportunities in working together. So the rest of this chapter focuses on the kinds of problems which commonly seem to confront people when they move to this new kind of teamwork, and it attempts to find ways round some of them.

In considering how additional people may best have their work organized in order to maximize their contribution it will help to look at some of the features of classroom organization and classroom dynamics which are going to be relevant to such an analysis. There is a large body of research available from which to draw.

We must remember that many of the extra people who are moving into classrooms are concerned with special educational needs. So, if we are to meet these needs in mainstream classrooms through the integration of the *staff* previously associated with 'special' children we need to outline what these needs might be. Some important special needs of children who are experiencing difficulties might be sketched out as follows: a need for regular practice; a need for distributed practice (i.e. frequent short doses of help are generally better than fewer longer sessions); a need for more prompting and more help[6].

All of these are difficult to provide; in fact, in large part they reduce to the need for more individual attention. But more individual attention is notoriously difficult to provide if we are also to provide the amount of attention we would wish for the main body of the class. This problem – the tension caused by having to do two things at once – is one that comes up time and again when thinking about meeting special needs in the mainstream.

So how might the class management literature be assessed with a view to finding out about and resolving such tensions in the teacher's role? It is the identification of such tensions which will be crucial for an appraisal of the possible contributions of additional people. For additional people do not merely bring extra pairs of hands: they bring a vast range of skills and expertise. Perhaps even more importantly, they may bring opportunities for a new dynamic within the classroom; previously held fundamentals about the use of space and time in the class will be altered by the presence of another person. Problems due to the adoption of a particular teaching style may be minimized when another person is in the class. If such altered dynamics do occur, it is important that the tension points in traditional dynamics (one person to one class) are explored in order that those extra people are involved most fully and most effectively.

In their chosen teaching strategy teachers appear to be choosing to sacrifice one important ingredient of classroom activity for another. It seems, for instance in looking at the ORACLE research, that choosing to give relatively large amounts of individual help has its consequence in the relatively low engagement of the class as a whole; on the other hand, those teachers who choose a strategy which enables high engagement among the class generally do not provide as much individual teaching[7].

Research from stables of different methodologies points to similar conclusions about the complexity of the teacher's task and the diversity of functions comprising it[8]. Running through Kounin's work is the notion of 'flow'. While experienced teachers acquire strategies for enabling them to maintain flow in a session, that is nevertheless an extremely difficult task. Many of the kinds of events which Kounin identifies as important for the teacher to respond to involve her attending to two things at once or require her being in two places at once. In the understanding of classroom processes that Kounin's work encourages is the realization that a multitude of events are *simultaneously* taking place in the classroom. As such, what emerges is the notion that the various functions which comprise the teacher's role are characterized not by synchrony; rather, the effective fulfilment of one of these functions often seems to preclude the effective fulfilment of another. If this is the case then there is a clear opportunity for the effectively organized use of additional help to reduce in size and scope some of these multifarious demands.

Out of all these elements which are important for the successful management of the classroom there seem to be two whose integrated provision it is very difficult to provide. Those two elements are individual teaching – valued so highly by Plowden and so necessary for children who are having problems – and maintenance of group engagement. It would appear that at the core of many of the 'flow' characteristics outlined by Kounin is the development by the teacher of strategies to reconcile the problems which arise out of the need to be attending to the individual while simultaneously attending to the needs of the rest of the class.

A system for organizing the work of extra people in the classroom can address an apparently irreconcilable conflict here. Clearly, having additional people in the classroom offers possibilities in terms of differentiating functions with each person meeting the differentiated function better than one person could singlehanded. Particularly interesting as far as the differentiation of the teaching process is concerned is the fact that properly co-ordinated efforts at teamwork addressing the significance of such differentiation may result in the team's efforts having a pay-off far higher than the summed efforts of its members working as individuals could provide.

A NEED FOR MODELS OF PERSONNEL ORGANIZATION?

With the best will in the world, it does not seem to be possible for a classteacher on her own adequately to meet the needs of children who are experiencing difficulty when they are part of a larger class. She will need effective assistance. Neither does it seem to be the case that involving additional people, trained or untrained, automatically helps the teacher in her task. Indeed, sometimes it actually appears to be the case that having extra people around inhibits the teacher in such a way that she spends more time thinking about what to do next with the 'visitor' than what to do next with the children[9].

Indeed, DeVault in a follow-up of personnel involvement in the various Project Follow Through curricula found that very little attention had been given to the organization or training of additional staff or volunteers in the classroom[10]. Even in highly funded projects those additional people had to fall back on modelling from the teacher's performance. The organization of their time was so lax that additional people, rather than freeing the teacher for more time with pupils, in fact typically freed her for more *non-teaching* activities. This finding is backed up again and again by findings on teaming in classrooms: organization tends to be lacking, and without the organization, the teaming process atrophies. Geen has shown how the process of teaming has fallen by the wayside in British classrooms after high hopes for it in the early 1970s[11]. Cohen showed that even in the more highly resourced classrooms of California, where additional people are found more frequently than in the UK, teaming might start after a burst of enthusiasm but then would wane without organization and support[12].

It is clearly important now to look at possible models for structuring the work of additional people. If the kind of differentiation in the teacher's role which has already been referred to can be added to such a system as well as consideration of how best to meet special needs, several important objectives will have simultaneously been met.

A MODEL FOR DISCUSSION – ROOM MANAGEMENT

There are limitless ways in which people's time and activity might be organized in the classroom. 'Room management' arose out of American work in settings for young children. The work was taken up in Great Britain by Porterfield, amongst others, who refined the ideas for use in institutions for mentally handicapped people[13]. A recently conducted pilot study of room management in a top primary school class has indicated that highly significant improvements in children's engagement may be achieved when this system of organization is employed as a basis for the structure of the activity of adults in the class[14].

At the core of room management lies the activity period, a specific period of time, usually of about an hour, when specific roles are allocated to the various people within the class. It suggests three separate roles are fulfilled: (i) an individual helper; (ii) an activity manager; and (iii) a mover. The individual helper(s) concentrates on taking individual children for short periods of teaching. Her work with those children will have been planned beforehand and she will work with a rota of children over the activity period. The activity manager(s) looks after the work of the rest of the children in the class, who are typically arranged into groups, with the aim of keeping the children engaged on the task in hand. This aim is facilitated through the planned activity of the children, which should be on areas of the curriculum that have already been covered though not necessarily mastered; children will therefore to a greater or lesser degree be consolidating on material and should require little individual help from the activity manager. Such a pattern of work amongst most children will enable the activity manager to effect a series of rapid contacts with this larger body. There is a large number of findings on the effective use of teacher attention in reducing inappropriate behaviour and increasing children's overall engagement[15]. In line with suggestions from these, the activity manager aims to maximize her contacts with those children who are working appropriately while prompting with the minimum attention those who are not.

The mover aims to maintain *flow* in the class by relieving the activity manager and the individual helper from distraction. She will, for instance, deal with interruptions, move equipment and sharpen pencils.

Looking back at our breakdown of classroom dynamics and at the learning needs of children who might be experiencing difficulty, we can see that this model has a number of attractions. In its method of providing individual help, it takes account of children's need for learning in short frequent doses. In its method of 'activity management' it says something about type of activity, both of children and adult, which will help if we are thinking primarily about the engagement of the group. And in the role of 'mover' we see someone who will be able to keep the flow going in a session.

There is room for wide adaptation of the system in such a way that the particular people participating in a class develop a unique solution to a unique set of circumstances. As children become more independent there is less need for the function of mover and some of her functions may be delegated to children within the group. If three people were available to work in, say, an upper junior classroom it may be possible to think of a configuration of two activity managers, each responsible for the work of certain groups, and one individual helper. Alternatively, those people may be arranged such that there are two individual helpers and one activity manager. The precise arrangement will depend on the needs of the class.

Case Study 2: a system of personnel organization in operation

Priory School is a large primary school with a reputation for liberal, innovative and child-centred education. It has a catchment which is generally considered to be one of the most difficult in its region. Partly to do with its tradition and its ethos, this was one of the first schools in the region to explore the possibilities in parental involvement. So the school opens its doors to parents not merely in the usual way (e.g. getting parents in to help with trips or to help with cookery) but also in more contentious ways: helping with reading in the class or helping with other 'academic' tasks.

It is within this context that Mrs Allen teaches her class of twenty-nine fourth-year juniors. Mrs Allen is a teacher of some twenty years' experience and as such she has developed a distinct, positive and effective style of classroom management. The children respect her. They work mainly independently on set tasks and are organized in groups by activity.

There are a number of children who are experiencing difficulty in Mrs Allen's class. Two of particular concern are Kevin and Karen. Although not a continuous nuisance in the class, Kevin is prone to sudden attacks of violent temper. Fortunately, such episodes are few but in the dormant phases of Kevin's classroom existence, he follows a solitary, sullen path, avoiding work wherever possible. Karen is very different. She is a withdrawn child who finds it very difficult to take in new information but will do her best to please, working to the best of her ability for long periods to very little effect.

It is a tribute to the relationship that the staff of the school has achieved in the locality that it has been possible to involve the mothers of these two children, not merely by discussing the children's difficulties with them but rather by bringing them into the classroom to become active participants in classroom life. At first these parents came into the classroom specifically to help their own children but after a time it was thought worthwhile experimenting with an alternative way of organizing their time, together with the time of an ancillary helper and the teacher in an alternative way.

It was felt that it would be worthwhile operating a system of room management for the times that these four adults would be in the class together. The system operated with one individual helper and three activity managers. The team comprised a teacher, a teaching assistant and two parents. For the hour that the operation ran the teacher acted as an individual helper, teaching new material to individual children, whilst the other adults worked as activity managers, concentrating on maintaining the focus of groups of children.

When the adults worked in this way the average engagement of the total group rose from around 60 per cent when people were not organized using room management to over 80 per cent when they were so organized. The most interesting point as far as children with special needs is concerned was that use of the system affected most beneficially the engagement of those children, including Kevin, who initially were least engaged.

Analysis of case study

A method such as this may not merely provide the framework for the involvement of parents in class. It may also provide the draft from which to proceed in deciding how two experienced teachers are going to work alongside each other. Particularly for those peripatetic teachers who are considering changing their style of work so that they are delivering their skills within the ordinary classroom alongside the classroom teacher, room management offers a useful model on which to base such a change in working practice.

How might this method be abbreviated, extended or adapted to fit the varying needs of different kinds of classroom? There is, for instance, the question of whether specialization of role is necessary or beneficial at all in certain circumstances. Studies of work-groups in industry appear to indicate that less rather than more specialization may be beneficial when people are working in groups[16]. This might also apply in the classroom, where it might be the case that in separating out the activities that different people do (as in room management) there is less opportunity for the adult to become aware of certain special needs, less of a family feeling amongst the group and perhaps less of a feeling of responsibility by adults for certain children.

Family grouping might overcome these problems. Such considerations may weigh particularly large in a group of very young children where a significant number of them are considered to have emotional problems. But it should be said that some of the additional people in the classroom may not feel they have the ability to take on the integrated functions implied by this kind of organization.

Overcoming some of the problems engendered by role delineation in meeting this need (though those problems should not be overstated in the classroom setting) is the possibility of rotating roles amongst the people present. Here at least the kind of dynamics which are generated by the same person always getting those jobs that are perceived to be menial or unpleasant are minimized. Rotation also allows for people to feel a sense of real participation by fulfilling a range of tasks.

Many themes are intertwined in any debate about the involvement of additional people in the classroom: many people will be eager to effect a greater participation by the community in the education of its children; there will be concerns over ways of enabling 'special' children to integrate; there will be concerns over the right of parents to be more involved in schools. All these themes raise a host of issues, which I have avoided in this chapter.

In choosing to focus primarily on organization I hope to have concentrated on the most important theme that teachers are currently confronting. The involvement of others in the classroom has already proceeded further than many might have expected: teachers are no longer asking *whether* other adults should be there alongside them; rather, they now ask *how* to make participation work.

There are no magic recipes in answer to the question *how*, because no two classrooms are the same. Neither can we say that the assortment of people who are finding their way into schools can be treated as a homogeneous block.

But there are common problems and opportunities in the moves which are currently occurring. If we examine what is currently going on in our classrooms, and if we examine the needs of all the children in them, there is at least the foundation for a more effective involvement of others in school. The onus is now not only on teachers to develop their own unique strategies for maximizing the contribution of those who, for whatever reason, are participating in the classroom. It is also on those who have the power to provide them with guidance, support and time. Teachers will require time for discussion, planning and monitoring. For without these, the ideals underpinning the moves to parental involvement and integration of children with special needs will never be realized.

REFERENCES AND NOTES

(1) Black, P. *Task Group or Assessment and Teaching: A Report*. London: DES, 1987.
(2) Bennett, N., Andreas, J., Hegarty, P. and Wade, B. *Open Plan Schools: Teaching, Curriculum, Design*. Windsor: NFER, 1980.
(3) Hargreaves, D. H. 'The occupational culture of teachers'. In Woods, P. (ed.) *Teacher Strategies: Explorations in the Sociology of the School*. London: Croom Helm, 1980.
(4) Thomas, G. 'Extra people in the primary classroom'. *Educational Research*, **29** (3), 173–181, 1987.
(5) Steiner, I. D. *Group Process and Productivity*. NY, USA: Academic Press, 1972.
(6) Thomas, G. 'Planning for support in the mainstream'. In Thomas,

G. and Feiler, A. (eds) *Planning for Special Needs*. Oxford, UK: Blackwell, 1988.

(7)   Galton, M. J., Simon, B. and Croll, P. *Inside the Primary Classroom*. London: Routledge & Kegan Paul, 1980.

(8)   Kounin, J. S. *Discipline and Group Management in Classrooms*. NY, USA: Holt, Rinehart & Winston, 1970; Brophy, J. 'Advances in teacher research'. *Journal of Classroom Interaction*, **15** (1), 1–7, 1979.

(9)   Thomas, G., 1987, op. cit.

(10)   DeVault, M. L., Harnischfeger, A. and Wiley, D. E. *Curricula, Personnel Resources and Grouping Strategies*. St. Ann, MO, USA: ML-GROUP for Policy Studies in Education, Central Midwestern Regional Lab., 1977.

(11)   Geen, A. G. 'Team teaching in the secondary schools of England and Wales'. *Educational Review*, **37** (1), 29–38, 1985.

(12)   Cohen, E. G. 'Problems and prospects of teaming'. *Educational Research Quarterly*, **1** (2), 49–63, 1976.

(13)   Porterfield, J., Blunden, R. and Blewitt, E. *Improving Environments for Profoundly Handicapped Adults: Establishing Staff Routines for High Client Engagement*. Cardiff: Mental Handicap in Wales Applied Research Unit, University of South Wales, Cardiff, 1977.

(14)   Thomas, G. 'Room management in mainstream education'. *Educational Research*, **27** (3), 186–94, 1985.

(15)   Becker, W. C., Madsen, C. H., Arnold, C. R. and Thomas, D. R. 'The contingent use of teacher attention and praise in reducing classroom behaviour problems'. *Journal of Special Education*, **1**, 287–307, 1967.

(16)   Hackman, J. R. and Oldham, G. R. *Work Redesign*. Reading, MA, USA: Addison-Wesley, 1980.

Chapter 5

The Teacher and the Ethos of the School

Kate Ashcroft

EDITOR'S COMMENT

It is a great temptation to believe in the simplicities of change, that directives will be carried out according to the amount of will-power, that policies work as planned. It is as great a temptation as to believe that what teachers tell their pupils is exactly what they learn. Those who wish to make an impact believe in the simplicity of action rather than recognize how difficult it is to change other people's behaviour, but it is only in understanding the more subtle forces at work that real change comes about.

There are mythologies about educational management, as if clear aims and objectives could be translated into instrumental changes, without the complexities of human suspicion, doubt and refusal to conform. A change in any organization, including as fragile a hegemony as a school, is always as subtle and slow to achieve as a shift in philosophy.

And yet there are great differences between individual schools. With the same type of catchment area, with similar resources, with similar structures, some schools, as research reported in this chapter reveals, help their children achieve much more than others. From the point of view of those who would wish to create unified standards, such differences between schools, implying poor performance in some, are little short of scandalous. They would wish schools to achieve similar standards – preferably high ones.

The problem is that differences between schools will not be overcome by the imposition of a common curriculum. As this chapter outlines, the differences between schools are far more subtle than the subject matter taught. The 'hidden curriculum' has for years been a major source of fascination, being the values and beliefs actually presented to the children; the outcome rather than the intention. Again, there is a distinction to be made between the articulated aims and the perceived belief, as between the 'delivered' curriculum and its reception.

The problem with a concept such as 'ethos' is that it seems at first vague, or ephemeral. And yet it is as powerful a reality as, say, the organization of the timetable. It includes the curriculum that exists outside formal subjects, the events that happen in lunch hours as well as lessons. The variables between schools are rarely to do with the choice of curriculum. They rest far more on styles of teaching and on a shared sense of purpose.

In a sense this chapter discusses not just the complexities of the classroom interaction but the hidden curriculum. It unearths some of the expectations which are made implicit by teachers, and shows that there is more to what happens in a classroom than children concentrating on the 'task at hand'. ■   (C.C.)

As soon as any visitor enters a school they will be aware of a feeling or atmosphere. Messages will be picked up from the state and style of the buildings, the arrangement of furnishings, the displays on the wall and labels and notices around the school. But the most significant messages will come from the behaviour of the people involved: from the welcome received from the staff, the demeanour of the children and the behaviour of staff and children towards each other. With further acquaintance, messages will be received about the quality of the teachers' attitude to parents, their expectations of children in terms of work and behaviour and numerous other aspects of school life.

Together these and many other messages will create a 'feeling' which is clearly recognized by all those involved in the school. This feeling may be described as the 'ethos' of the school, although people working in the school may characterize it in many different ways.

The term 'ethos' thus describes an aspect of school life, the reality and importance of which will be recognized by most people who have been involved in schooling. However, the 'reality' of the ethos of a school is essentially a social construction. This raises issues which will be considered in this chapter. Ethos involves a climate that permeates and affects all aspects of the school. What then are the ingredients which together create this climate? Does the answer lie in the relationships between the people who work in the school, the head, the teachers, the children, ancillary staff and visitors? What influences do the physical surroundings, the material resources available, the school's location, the Local Education Authority, have on the school? Do wider factors such as the national economic and political situation or the prevailing social and educational ideologies also have significant effects?

WHY IS ETHOS IMPORTANT?

Perhaps one of the most influential pieces of research into the concept of 'ethos' was undertaken by Rutter *et al.* during the 1970s[1]. This was a longitudinal study of 5485 children in the Inner London Educational Authority (ILEA) who were followed from their primary schools through five years of secondary schooling. They found that the differences in the schools' intakes could not explain the differences between outcomes when the children were fourteen. Schools with similar intakes seemed to produce very different results. The Rutter team put these differences in outcome down to differences in 'ethos' among the schools.

More effective schools appear to be those which function as a coherent whole, with staff at all levels supporting each other and working towards shared academic and social goals. In such schools, senior staff give a clear lead and at the same time teachers feel their views are represented.

Thus, Rutter's work indicates that the ethos of a school is important because it (or the combined effects of factors contributing to it) is positively related to educational outcomes.

Unfortunately Rutter's 'outcomes' do not necessarily define the purposes of schooling and some outcomes such as examination performance and rates of delinquency may have little relevance to the primary schools. Others may not be among the priorities even of secondary schools. The Rutter research did not explore processes such as curriculum development or the willingness of the staff and head to innovate. In the more child-centred primary sector these may be more important aspects. In addition, in a primary school the children themselves may have a greater effect on the 'ethos' of the school than Rutter suggests. However, despite these and other criticisms, Rutter found much evidence that some schools seem to have consistently better outcomes than others and this is largely a result of shared rules, standards and values of those within the school.

The findings of Reynolds support the view that a positive climate is an important factor in school effectiveness[2]. He found that the school's policy towards children is of central importance. A climate where children feel they are part of decision making, the school's social structure, rather than being coerced, produces higher educational achievement. In such schools, teachers value and reward academic achievement and 'humanistic' activity.

Brookover *et al.* also found that attitudes to children are influencial on academic achievement[3]. In effective schools there is an assumption that the children are willing and able to learn and very few are 'written off'. In an ineffective school the same children would be classified as slow and unable to learn:

> We therefore conclude that a school's social climate and the instructional behaviours associated with it are more direct causal links in the production of achievement behaviour in reading and mathematics than socio-economic and racial variables.

A criticism of these studies when applying their findings in the primary school context is that much of the work was undertaken in secondary schools. Outcomes that were measured in some cases seem 'mechanistic' (perhaps because they are easier to measure) and outside of the more 'romantic' primary tradition and concerns. However, there has been a more recent project looking at the effectiveness of 50 ILEA primary schools which discovered that some schools were more effective than others in promoting pupils' learning and development, and also in catering for particular groups of children such as boys or girls, and children from different social classes and ethnic groups[4]. In the study, account was taken of variations in the pupils' background. Twelve factors were found to influence the effectiveness of the school. The schools which produced a positive ethos had the following characteristics:

1. Purposeful leadership by the headteacher. Headteachers were actively involved in the school's work, without exacting *total* control.
2. Involvement of the deputy head. Headteachers shared and delegated some of their responsibilities. Frequent absence of the deputy was detrimental to pupil progress.
3. Involvement of teachers. Teachers were involved in cur-

riculum planning, guideline development and decision making.

4. Consistency among teachers. Teachers were consistent in the use of guidelines.

5. Structured sessions. Teachers organized pupils' work programmes and gave them plenty to do. Once work had been allocated, pupils were encouraged to work independently.

6. Intellectually challenging teaching. Teachers used higher-order questions and statements, encouraging pupils to solve problems and use creative imagination.

7. Work-centred environment. Classrooms were busy and purposeful with teachers spending time discussing the content of work rather than routine issues. Pupils appeared to enjoy their work and were keen to start new work. Classrooms were reasonably quiet and without excessive movement.

8. Limited focus within sessions. Teachers concentrated on one or two curriculum areas in any session. All pupils were not, however, doing the same work and teachers geared the work to pupils' needs.

9. Maximum communication between pupils and teachers. This was achieved by the teacher talking more often to the whole class or groups rather than to individuals. This enabled 'higher order' communication to occur more often.

10. Record keeping. Teachers kept good records of planning and assessment of pupils' personal, social and development work.

11. Parental involvement. Schools had an informal open-door policy with parents helping in the classroom and on visits and regular meetings organized to discuss pupils' progress. Parents were involved in pupils' educational development. The mere fact of having a formal parent–teacher association was not sufficient to promote a positive ethos.

12. Positive climate. The emphasis within the schools was on praise and encouragement rather than criticism and punishment. There was firm but fair classroom management with teachers having a positive attitude to their classes and taking an interest in all aspects of the children.

They organized trips and lunchtime and after-school clubs. The teachers had good working conditions and timetabled non-teaching periods.

The researchers point out that these factors cannot constitute a complete 'recipe' for promoting pupil learning but may provide a framework within which school effectiveness and its relationship to ethos may be considered.

It is interesting to note that many of the factors identified in the ILEA study are similar to those found by earlier studies to contribute to the ethos of a school. This is important because effectiveness may require a different definition at primary level and the definitions may change alongside altering perceptions of the role of the primary school. At this level it may be necessary, as Golby says, to ask new questions such as whether the school's purposes are in line with those of parents, pupils and society[5]. It is not possible to assume that the conventional school curriculum is consistent with those purposes. Gray points out other questions that are relevant in the primary school context[6]. For instance, measures of effectiveness can only be used with confidence if schools are stable from year to year and they enable educational practitioners to identify more effective schools. We need to know whether the effects of 'ethos' are greater or less at primary level. It is important to know how the 'ethos' of a school becomes established and whether, as Frances believes, process interacts with outcomes to produce a spiral effect, rather than a directly causal effect on outcomes[7].

What does seem apparent from the research referred to above and from work by others such as McDill, Webber, Madden and Brookover and Lezotte, is that there are combinations of factors, which may be termed 'ethos', that have profound effects on pupil performance[8].

In teasing out the factors that affect the ethos of schools it is apparent that management has a great influence. Central to this is the relationship that exists between the headteacher and staff. Indeed the DES Report of 1977 states that the headteacher is the most important factor in the climate of a school[9].

HOW DOES MANAGEMENT CONTRIBUTE TO ETHOS?

Research indicates that effective headteachers are sympathetic, empathetic and accessible. Nias found that such headteachers set clear aims for the school that are subject to negotiation within limits[10]. The capacity to create cohesion and to support and encourage individuals is essential. This is likely to be enhanced by the head's own high standard of personal commitment and professional competence.

Simon identifies two leadership styles which may be adopted by headteachers[11]. The first involves the use of influence. Such headteachers seek to understand problems thoroughly in order to arrive at the right line of action. This involves an appeal to expertise and obtaining the consent of staff to proposed developments. The second involves the use of control, the exercise of authority to obtain the acquiescence of staff through a mixture of threat and persuasion. Management that relies on control may divide staff and invite confrontation or passive resistance. Bolam and Pratt point out that controllers may adopt strategies that involve the use of incentives as well as sanctions[12]. If compliance is forced it may result in low staff morale and a lack of effort. Such a headteacher is likely to lose the confidence of staff. Ballinger found that at the extreme such headteachers may use autocratic strategies of lying, rigging agendas or altering information in order to deny or exclude opposing ideas[13].

Blake and Mouton found that school managements may be more or less focused on social satisfaction or task achievement[14]. School managements which focus on neither may be described as impoverished. Those that focus on social satisfaction to the exclusion of task achievement may be described as 'Country Clubs', pleasant places to work in but not very effective. Those that focus exclusively on task achievement do so at the expense of the social and emotional development of teachers and children. The ideal, of course, is to focus on both aspects. Most schools focus more on one aspect or the other at different times.

Miles's model of 'organizational health' sought to identify dimensions of effective management[15]. He grouped ten dimensions of organizational health under three main headings. Two of these, task-centred and maintenance needs, are closely related to those identified by Blake and Mouton but he adds a third, growth and changefulness. Miles's dimensions are as follows:

Task-centred

(a) Goal focus: goals should be clear, accepted, realistic and achievable.
(b) Optimal power equalization: teachers motivated by feelings of involvement and competence.
(c) Communication adequacy: vertical and horizontal lines of communication should be open, easy and distortion free.

Maintenance needs

(a) Cohesiveness: clear sense of identity which is attractive to teachers.
(b) Morale: well-being, laughter, lack of stress.
(c) Resource utilization: resources should be co-ordinated so that teachers are working hard, in jobs they suit but are not stressed.

Growth and changefulness

(a) Innovativeness: growth and development, increase in range of school's and teacher's activities.
(b) Autonomy: staff should respond to, but not be dictated to, by pressures from outside.
(c) Problem-solving adequacy: problems identified, solved and evaluated with minimum stress.
(d) Adaption: strength and stability in order to allow for faster change.

It is often assumed that a headteacher likely to foster organizational health might be described as democratic. However, Crick believes that democracy does not provide a good model for effective management[16]. Its meaning is too uncertain. It may mean majority rule, or the will of the staff, or 'one person–one vote' or the pursuit of equality. It is not a suitable model for school management, where all decisions cannot be taken by the whole staff. In a democracy, general interests may be taken into account but minority interests may be ignored. To manage well, headteachers may have to go against popular opinion and desirable goals may be mutually exclusive. Crick saw a political style of leadership as more appropriate, in which teachers' and children's interests are represented and communication is open but where the headteacher may take a wider view.

Hoyle described the micropolitics of school management in which groups within the staff may co-operate to achieve a common goal. Such groupings may be *ad hoc* or formal and may be committed to preserving the *status quo*[17]. Such groupings may lead to the 'dark underworld' of illegitimate micropolitics which include power broking and closed political processes. Marsh and Olsen describe how decisions may be made before consultation and negotiation and history 'rewritten' to make the process appear more rational[18].

Handy describes how groups, whether legitimate or illegitimate, provide a psychological home for individuals by providing institutional and individual functions[19]. Individual functions include the satisfaction of social needs, such as self-esteem, support and sharing. Institutional functions include management needs such as problem-solving, information collection and processing co-ordination, commitment, negotiation and enquiry. Beneficial functioning of groups occurs where relations between individuals at all levels are good. Ideas are better evaluated and involvement is increased. This can lead to a positive cycle being established where greater productivity leads to more satisfaction, which in turn leads to still greater productivity.

In this process Richardson emphasized the importance of open and honest communication[20]. This is only possible if the headteacher communicates trust in the teachers' abilities to educate children. When this trust is built up teachers can risk exposing problems and revealing weaknesses and so develop their skills. A warm and accepting atmosphere is necessary before staff can examine what is good and bad in their school. The fostering of delusions, or suffocation of conflicting ideas beneath a veneer of politeness, will tend to mask problems. This can produce the problem of the preservation of harmony becoming an end in itself, resulting in a resistance to any change in the *status quo*. Beeby pointed out the importance of an honest questioning and examination of behaviour and values that had to be taken for granted[21]. Planning in education is not purely objective but involves value systems and attitudes which need to be discussed. Having been implemented, change should be subject to criticism and feedback.

This is only possible where teachers feel their interests are taken into account and there is communication between all levels of staff. An autocratic headteacher will invite confrontation or passive resistance. Such a head will be denied feedback from the teachers in the school and the opportunity to improve planning in the light of experience. The teachers are unlikely to experience support from the headteacher or the satisfaction of a task well done with the consequence of low morale. The headteacher's role within an effective school is thus very demanding and diffuse, in order to produce a climate where problems may be solved in co-operation. The headteacher must initiate change and motivate staff by example and consideration.

WHAT FACTORS INHIBIT THE DEVELOPMENT OF A POSITIVE ETHOS?

I have discussed research findings which identify positive and negative factors within schools which affect the development of ethos. However, I would argue that in today's economic and political climate there are many pressures outside schools' control which may inhibit the development of positive ethos.

Education takes place in a politicized context, with all the implications that has for accountability. In the context of the 1988 Education Reform Act schools can no longer (if they ever could) ignore the community in which they work. Parents will be closely involved in the management of schools and decisions over opting out. In addition schools will operate in a 'market place' where they must attract 'customers' and satisfy those they have already attracted. This is, however, not just a new phenomenon. Government reports from Plowden[22] through to recent reports such as Warnock[23] have emphasized the need for parental involvement in primary schools. This has led to a much greater openness but also to the development of tensions. The school has to become more explicit about its aims, and these may be challenged by parents who do not feel them to be in tune with their needs and purposes. Problems may become more acute with the publication of schools' assessment results. At the same time as schools are responding to parents' interests and needs, they are under pressure from government and local authority expectations. Those of central government have become very detailed and explicit and may conflict in some respects with its previous policies and philosophy of the Local Education Authority. The resolution of these tensions can lead to real progress, but in order for this to happen the pacing and timing of change needs careful consideration. Unfortunately this does not always appear to be the case. Even before the Education Act headteachers and teachers felt pressured by the sheer number of new initiatives that they were invited, or pressed to participate in. These arrived from a variety of sources, each convinced that their concerns should receive priority. The HMI document on the curriculum from 5 to 16 years states[24]:

> schools will necessarily have to take account of the policy decisions of LEAs and central government and of the expectations of parents, employers and the community at large . . . schools also have to respond to social changes, to the impact of technology and to changing patterns of employment . . . schools have to take account of the varying concerns of all those who 'use' the system, in ways which outline the extringencies of the moment.

This thinking has been implemented by the Act. Such consideration and accountability is a tall order, especially as many of the interest groups will have conflicting concerns and requirements. At a time of low morale and declining resources the sheer weight of these demands can have profoundly inhibiting effects on the climate of schools and consequently for school effectiveness. The government in its document, *Better Schools* states[25]:

> the Government's view, following HMI reports, is that a significant number of teachers are performing below the standard required to achieve the planned objectives of schools.

Such statements, even though true in specific instances, may have a harmful effect on teacher morale, especially given the large number of aspects that schools are expected to take action on, some required by law and others a priority by influential pressure groups. The problem which confronts schools and teachers is not in the first instance the truth or otherwise of the various criticisms (many of them may indeed be true in particular situations), or the value or otherwise of the various initiatives (many of which may be very worthwhile) but rather how to handle the volume of criticism and initiatives without damaging the morale of teachers which underpins the successful ethos of schools.

There are, unfortunately, no simple solutions to these problems. Part of the answer may, however, lie in the work that teachers do together in defining a framework for the consideration of problems and issues.

WHAT ACTION CAN SCHOOLS TAKE TO DEVELOP A POSITIVE ETHOS?

The ethos of a school is in large part determined by the values of those working within it. It therefore becomes necessary for teachers to discuss and analyse those values before priorities for action can properly be defined. It is important to define values within a school, because ethos is the expression of these values.

There are questions which are fundamental to any such consideration. The first is the definition of the nature of teaching. It may not be assumed that all staff share the same view of what constitutes teaching. Fox discovered that teachers defined their purposes in teaching very differently[26]. He grouped these definitions into four main categories:

1. Transfer. In this model teaching is seen as the process of transferring knowledge from one person (the teacher) to another (the child). The child is seen as an empty vessel and if knowledge fails to be transferred the problem tends to be seen as residing in the child (i.e. the vessel is leaky).
2. Shaping. Teaching is the process of moulding children to a predetermined pattern. Children are taught skills and ways of behaving which are viewed as useful in themselves. The child's interests and motives are only important in so far as they interfere with the moulding process.
3. Travelling. In this model teaching is seen as a matter of guiding children through subject matter. The subject is viewed as an exciting and sometimes difficult terrain to be explored.
4. Growing. The focus of teaching is on the child's intellectual physical and emotional development. The teacher's job is to provide the situation and experience to assist the child in this development. This is a child-centred model, in which the subject matter is important, not as an end in itself, but only in as much as it meets the child's needs and is in the child's interests (this may not always be the same as what interests the child).

Each of these models has important implications for teacher action and concern and hence for the ethos of the school. Many primary school staffs would, I suspect, define their purposes in terms of 'growing'. In this case there are important factors that arise and need to be discussed in order to develop a philosophy and action that will promote a positive ethos. A staff which has defined its values and developed a philosophy of teaching will need to consider the practical implications. Below I have outlined five aspects which may be considered.

Evaluation and record keeping. If each child's interests and needs are to be met these must be accurately determined, monitored and recorded. Reliance solely on the teacher's intuition and perception is likely to produce an inaccurate picture, and a more homogeneous one than exists in reality. Teachers will therefore need to share their knowledge of individual children and together devise methods of collecting data on individual children, for instance through observation schedules, checklists, analysing children's work, individual questioning and group discussion. Records of children's development, needs and interests will have to be constantly updated. In this the TGAT report[27] may have provided a useful way forward – but not if teachers 'teach to the tests' in order to protect themselves from criticism and fail to use the results for diagnostic purposes to improve children's learning experiences and develop their teaching.

Teaching and learning methods. In order to meet the range of individual children's needs for intellectual, physical and emotional development teachers may have to extend their range of teaching and learning methods. Many teachers rely on a relatively limited repertoire of teaching methods which are unlikely to suit the stage of development and learning style of each individual in their class, or even the different needs of any particular child meeting different subject matter or in various situations. There will therefore be a need for teachers to share expertise.

Planning. If the child rather than the subject matter is to be the focus of teaching, the planning of the curriculum purely in terms of subject matter will no longer be adequate. HMI[28] suggest that the curriculum should also be analysed in terms of skills, attitudes, concepts and knowledge. There is concern that the emerging reports of the national curriculum subject working parties pay insufficient attention to attitudes. The national curriculum may help to ensure continuity and coherence within the subjects but teaching may become fragmented and opportunities to reinforce learning across its curriculum may be ignored. In addition, the needs of children who do not acquire skills, concepts and knowledge in a linear way will need to be met. Teachers will need support from each other to analyse what they are doing in order to maximize the benefits of the national curriculum and minimize its defects. Curriculum planning and analysis in these terms will be new to many teachers and is likely to be difficult. Again teachers are more likely to produce flexible and effective plans which will meet the needs of all the individual children if they support and advise each other in this endeavour.

Organization.   In order to meet the needs of individual children within the school, it is necessary that the staff group examines the way people, space and time are organized, including looking at them from the child's point of view. In many schools routines have been built up that may interfere with the child's needs and interests. Space may need to be reorganized to allow a wider variety of children's activity to co-exist. Time should also be considered, both in terms of the 'class' day and the individual child's day. For instance it is not uncommon for infant schools to 'work' in the morning and 'choose' in the afternoon on the grounds that children are fresher in the morning. Assumptions such as this need questioning. What 'hidden' messages are being conveyed about the relative importance of different types of activity? Are the children's needs for changes in the pace of activity within sessions being met? When teachers examine the use of time as experienced by individual children they are often surprised. A child with learning difficulties may be in a class where a wide variety of activities take place, but day after day he works so painfully slowly that he never moves on from his written work. How are this child's needs for social learning, creative expression and successfully meeting a challenge to be satisfied?

Relationships.   A definition of teaching which is concerned with children's intellectual, physical and emotional development, implies a consideration of the whole child. Children cannot be viewed as *tabulae rasae* when they come to school. This has implications for relationships with the community which the child comes from and especially with parents. A comparison of roles of the teacher and the parent will soon reveal much overlap. The parent and the teacher will have much that is useful to offer each other. School staffs who adopt this model will have to analyse carefully their policy towards parents to discover if it is as open as possible and genuinely equal and two-way. Other schools are coming to realize the importance of partnerships with parents after the Education Reform Act more painfully. There are, however, more important reasons for the involvement of parents than the Act. Without a developing relationship with parents, teachers will be less able to understand children's cultural background and treat them with the respect they merit. Through this understanding teachers can avoid simplistic labels and stereotypes, value minority customs and focus upon what cultures have in common rather than on differences and problems. The school's policy towards children will also need to be examined to ensure that all children's needs for social satisfaction and task achievement are met and special skills or talents nurtured. The actions of teachers will need to be analysed and questioned – for instance it may be necessary to examine the experience of education offered to girls and boys respectively or children from different cultural backgrounds. In order to cater for children's emotional needs the question of motivation will need to be addressed. For instance the use of positive reinforcement may need to be monitored. Unfortunately, many primary teachers use criticism more often than praise. It may be necessary to instigate a policy of finding something of value to praise for each child every day. Methods of control by criticism may be replaced by finding the child who is working well and praising him. Work by Blanchard and Johnson points to the effectiveness of a policy of systematically 'catching children being good', which creates a more positive ethos[29]. The type of relationships which underpin a 'growing' model of teaching can be very problematic to teachers. There is an implication of more equality between teacher, parent and child. The classroom is no longer the teacher's territory and she may have to accept parents' freer access to the room or to the child's work. In this process the support of other teachers is likely to be very necessary.

The model presented here emphasizes words such as 'share', 'support', 'collaboration' and 'relationships'. This reflects the view that the development of ethos cannot be a 'top down' activity decided by a government or the headteacher and implemented by the staff, but rather requires continual discussion and honest examination by everyone working in the school.

A MODEL FOR CONTINUING GROWTH

Once a school staff has examined the purposes of teaching and the implications of these purposes it may be useful to consider what model of the teacher is appropriate. One model that may prove useful is that of the 'reflective teacher'. Zeichner drew on Dewey's qualities as prerequisite for reflective action in his definition[30]:

1. Openmindedness. This implies the consideration of more than one side to any question and a recognition of the problematic nature of decision making.
2. Responsibility. The assessment of long- and short-term consequences of action – looking beyond immediate utility to the consideration of underlying principles and values. Such teachers look beyond a consideration of 'what works' towards consideration of *worthwhileness*.
3. Wholeheartedness. Openmindedness and responsibility being central components in the life of the teacher and the school.

In order to implement the 'group' philosophy outlined earlier in the chapter a school staff moving towards such a model would need critically to examine shared assumptions and values and analyse those of others involved in education. Such an examination would enable teachers to assess the worthwhileness of the various initiatives emerging from within and outside of the school and establish clear priorities for action, within a framework of practical and ethical considerations. Zeichner and Teitelbaum state that[31]:

> to argue that classroom practice must be divorced from its moral roots . . . is an essentially conservative stance and serves to strengthen those institutional forces that prevent our moral aspirations from being realised.

A self-renewing, forward-moving primary school must therefore analyse the worthwhileness of its present position and of any new initiatives. A quotation from Zeichner and Teitelbaum illustrates this point[32]:

> What is hoped for, instead, is to create a situation where (teachers) maintain more of a balance between the arrogance that blindly rejects and the servility that blindly receives . . . Let this debate . . . be over what is the *right* course of action and not merely the most efficient.

The model implies a deep concern with underlying principles and values. Openmindedness implies a consideration of, and dialogue with, all those with an interest in schooling. For this to be possible staff will need to consider problems of access and methods of keeping themselves informed of perspectives and developments in the community and the wider debate on education. With such knowledge teachers can make the kind of decisions that will help the school move towards a more positive ethos.

Many simple questions are posed about education, but unfortunately there are no simple answers. Berlak and Berlak found it difficult to describe the reality of classroom situations in British schools until they invented a 'dilemma' language[33]. The implication of their work is that most of the decisions that teachers make have costs as well as benefits and seldom is it possible to have the best of both worlds. Dilemmas that teachers face include: how to treat children as 'whole people' rather than students; what control children should have over what they do; when and to what standard; the nature of knowledge, motivation and childhood; and problems of the allocation of resources and justice. Teachers have to decide whether all children should be treated equally in the interests of fairness or how differences in ability, interests and culture should be catered for.

Teachers moving towards a 'reflective teacher' model need to analyse patterns of resolution of these and other dilemmas. Questions should be addressed as to whether individual or groups of children receive differences in quality and quantity in the allocation of attention and time and how these differences are 'merited' (for instance personal traits, cultural disadvantage or social benefit). Consideration might be given to differing patterns of resolution in differing subject matter or with different groups of children and the hidden messages about values such patterns may convey.

In the consideration of these questions two-way communication with parents and the community is essential. The Secretary of

State for Education in a speech in 1986 stated the need for primary school teachers to communicate

> their achievements, their aims, their good practice, in terms which other people, especially parents can relate to . . . Education needs the intelligent support of its customers. Schools which do not have the support of children's other and first educators – their parents – put at risk what they are trying to achieve for these children. It is vital that parents and teachers understand, and respect, each other's aims.

This already represented good practice in many primary schools. Had it been the case in the others, many features of the Education Reform Act might have been eliminated. The ethos of a school is to a large extent the manifestation of its values. Values do not exist in isolation. They are socially defined. It therefore becomes necessary for teachers to examine their own values, to take into account the values of parents and the community and to consider and communicate the implications of this examination for school and classroom practice and the education of children.

The 'reflective teacher' model adds a further dimension to the process of collaboration and communication which is necessary for the development of a positive ethos. It provides a framework for the analysis of dilemmas inherent in action and its consequences and of the influences and pressures every school is subject to. It prevents an acceptance of the *status quo*, or change for change's sake and allows for a developing ethos which is stimulating for everyone involved in the life of the school and prevents the stultifying effect of an ethos developed for a different time which may be unsuited to today's purposes.

REFERENCES

(1)   Rutter, M. *15,000 Hours: Secondary Schools and Their Effects on Children*. Wells, UK: Open Books, 1979.
(2)   Reynolds, D. 'The search for effective schools'. In Smetherham, D. (ed.) *School Organisation*, Vol. 3, No. 2. London: Falmer Press, 1982.
(3)   Brookover, W., Beady, C., Flood, P., Schweitzer, S. and Wisenbaker, I. *School Social Systems and Student Achievement: Schools Can Make a Difference*. Cambridge, MA, USA: Ballenger, 1979.
(4)   ILEA. *The Junior School Project*. London: ILEA, 1986.
(5)   Golby, M. 'On from Rutter: researching educational effectiveness'. In *The Rutter Research*. Univ. of Exeter School of Education, 1979.

(6) Gray, J. 'Towards effective research: problems and progress in British research'. *British Educational Research Journal*, **7**, 1, 1981.

(7) Frances, H. 'A question of method'. In Tizard, B. *et al. Fifteen Thousand Hours: A Discussion*. University of London Institute of Education, 1980.

(8) *Cited in* Wragg, E. C. 'Theory into practice: implications for schools and Local Education Authorities'. In *The Rutter Research*. Univ. of Exeter School of Education, 1979.

(9) DES. *Education in Schools*. London: HMSO, 1977.

(10) Nias, J. 'Leadership styles and job satisfaction in primary schools'. In Bush, T., Glatter, R., Goody, J. and Riches, C. *Approaches to School Management*. London: Harper & Row, 1980.

(11) Simon, H. A. *Administrative Behaviour*. London: Collier/Macmillan, 1957.

(12) Bolam, R. and Pratt, S. *The Management of Innovation in Schools*. London: Open University Press, 1976.

(13) Ballinger, E. 'The politics of establishing an innovatory management role'. *Educational Management and Administration*, **10** (2), 1982.

(14) Blake, R. R. and Mouton, J. S. *The Versatile Manager: A Grid Profile*. Homewood, Il, USA: R. D. Irwin, 1982.

(15) Miles, M. B. 'Planned change and organisational health: figure and ground'. In Carlson, R. O. *Change Processes in Public Schools*. Centre for the Advanced Study of Educational Administration, University of Oregon Press, 1965.

(16) Crick, B. *In Defence of Politics*. London: Penguin, 1982.

(17) Hoyle, E. 'Micropolitics of educational organisations'. *Educational Management and Administration*, **10** (2), 1982.

(18) Marsh, J. G. and Olsen, J. P. *Ambiguity and Choice in Organisations*. Bergen: Universitetsforlaget, 1976.

(19) Handy, C. B. 'On the working of groups'. In Bush *et al. Approaches to School Management*. London: Harper & Row, 1980.

(20) Richardson, E. *The Teacher, the School and the Task of Education*. London: Heinemann, 1973.

(21) Beeby, C. E. *Planning and the Educational Administrator*. UNESCO: IIEP, 1966.

(22) DES. *Children and Their Primary Schools* (Plowden report). London: HMSO, 1967.

(23) DES. *Education of Handicapped Children and Young People: Special Educational Needs* (Warnock report). London: HMSO, 1978.

(24) DES. *The Curriculum from 5–16*. Curriculum Matters 2, HMI Series. London: HMSO, 1985, p. 6.

(25) DES. *Better Schools*. London: HMSO, 1985, p. 11.

(26) Fox, D. 'Personal theories of teaching'. *Studies in Higher Education*, **8** (2), 1983.

(27) DES. *Task Group on Assessment and Testing: A Report*. By P. J. Black *et al.* London: HMSO, 1988.

(28) HMI/DES, 1985, op. cit.

(29) Blanchard, K. and Johnson, S. *The One Minute Manager*. London: Fontana, 1983.
(30) Zeichner, K. M. 'Reflective teaching and field based experience in teacher education'. *Interchange,* **12** (4), 1–22, 1982.
(31) Zeichner, K. M. and Teitelbaum, K. 'Personalised and inquiry-oriented teacher education: an analysis of two approaches to the development of curriculum for field based experiences'. *Journal of Education for Teaching,* **8** (2), 95–117, 1982.
(32) Ibid, pp. 112–3.
(33) Berlak, A. and Berlak, H. *Dilemmas of Schooling: Teaching and Social Change*. London: Methuen, 1981.

Chapter 6

Relationships and Rules in the Classroom

Andrew Pollard

EDITOR'S COMMENT

As counsellors and others concerned with individual development know, relationships between any two human beings are complex, whether in an everyday or formal setting. There is an art to helping others articulate what they want to say; an art to listening and an art in advice. But if interpersonal dialogues are complicated, what do we make of the performance of teachers in classrooms? The teacher is creating relationships with, say, thirty individuals at the same time. She needs to know, when a child calls out, whether to ignore him, respond to him, divert his attention, cajole him, or discipline him, and then work out the best way to do so, according to his temperament, personality, mood, needs and circumstances. And this is a simple case.

It is difficult to explain actions which are so complex that they have to be instinctive. Rather than try to clarify the characteristics of behaviour it is perhaps more practical to simplify them into alternatives or dichotomies. But it is not always helpful if we see the role of the teacher either as the awe-inspiring aloof figure dispensing erudition, or as the kindly person creating warm and secure relationships. As in any position which involves one person in a relationship with many, the contraries which make up the two sides of individual charisma – distance and friendliness – are very important.

Such a tension between formality and approachability, as this chapter shows, can also be seen in terms of 'discipline'. On the one hand there is an acceptance of the need for rules, which need to be simply followed. On the other is a desire that the rules make sense to each individual, that they contain a series of separate validities. This tension is not just true of the school as a whole but, in a more subtle way, of the classroom.

The question of rules and control is not one that disappears once a particular pattern is established. Within the 'framework' there are changes of mood which are undetected. The teacher, for example, still fulfils a certain role in the eyes of children whatever she might be feeling at the time, even if she feels that one lesson has been far more successful than another. And even if the teacher attempts to be as informal as possible in her questions, to invite original and idiosyncratic responses, the children will still treat her questioning as formal, and try to guess what it is she expects them to say.

The concept of ethos is important because it shows that you cannot measure by measurement alone, that there are matters to understand, and change, not by a stroke of the pen, but by an understanding of the individuality of human nature. In so many recent research studies on the inner worlds of school, there are clear indications how they can improve. We do have an instinct of what makes one school better than another. The question remains whether this accumulated evidence will make any difference to the practitioners themselves, to those who control schools or to those who feel they know all about schools without needing to enter them. For as the concept of ethos makes clear, it is the individual personality that counts. Those who understand the theory might not be able to change; those who know the answers to schools will refuse to change. And yet the possibility of actions which profoundly affect schools is clearly before us. ■   (C.C.)

———————————

For many years achieving a high quality in classroom relationships has been regarded by many teachers as an essential and integral part of 'good' primary school practice. Indeed, such concern about relationships contributed, particularly in the post-Plowden years (since 1967), to the establishment of a 'child-centred ideology' in the primary schools of England and Wales[1].

Since the mid-1970s critiques of such ideas and of the associated practice have gradually gathered strength and have culminated in the Education Reform Act of 1988. This legislation is intended to provide a more 'rigorous' curriculum with programmes of study in identified subject areas and associated assessment of attainment targets, to be reported to parents of primary aged children. Schools and teachers are to be made more accountable through an increase in the powers of governing bodies together with an increase in parental representation, through open enrolment and through the publication of the whole-school results of assessments for 11-year-olds (with a recommendation that this also be done at age 7). As Tomlinson has commented, 'the objectives are to create a social market in education. . . . Education needs to be seen as a commodity to be purchased and consumed'[2].

Clearly, such changes in the context in which teachers work are likely to have a dramatic impact. It remains to be seen how they will affect that central teacher concern with classroom relationships – a theme to which I will return at the end of the chapter.

My interest in classroom relationships goes back to my first experience of teaching in 1972. It was soon clear that 'discipline' and classroom order could only be maintained with the co-operation of the children, for, were they mindful to do so, they could undercut my clumsy efforts at control with ease. I also discovered that developing a close rapport with children felt good – it gave me pleasure and a sense of fulfilment. These realizations have come over many years and have been refined by a number of detailed studies of classrooms and schools in which I have used ethnographic methods to gather data on teachers' and children's perspectives and to observe them in action[3]. Here I want to focus on one part of this work and try, somewhat tentatively, to develop it a little more.

The chapter is particularly concerned with classroom rules about behaviour. In the first part, the processes which contribute to the formation of classroom relationships are briefly described and this is followed by a more detailed discussion of rules and the concept of 'rule-frame'. One aspect of this, the question of the content of rules, is the subject of the next section and I illustrate some links between teachers' immediate classroom concerns and classroom rules. In a final section I consider some wider social implications of this analysis and, in particular, the extent to which it reinforces the argument that schooling can act to reinforce social divisions and to produce social control[4]. I will conclude by reflecting on the possible implications of the Education Reform Act.

RELATIONSHIPS AND RULE-FRAME

The concept which, in my view, best describes the social climate and nature of teacher–child relationships is that of 'working consensus'. This concept derives from an analysis of classrooms which recognizes the different power resources of the teachers and the taught, together with their particular perspectives and interests, and seeks to identify patterns in the ways in which they interact[5]. Teachers and children are seen as being engaged in continuous processes of negotiation. They each act strategically to cope with the difficulties which they face in classrooms but, as part of such actions, they are also often involved in exchange. This arises because the 'self' of each individual is seen as being vulnerable in classroom life. Teachers are acutely conscious of the numbers of children who may challenge their control, whilst children are very aware of the power of the teacher to assess and evaluate. Thus both teachers and children recognize that the other has the power to threaten their classroom fulfilment and even their 'survival' if provoked. A working consensus represents a situation in which each party learns to recognize and accept the legitimate interests of the other – in a sense there seems to be a mutual exchange of dignity. Such a consensus is usually negotiated during the first few weeks with a new class and, in many instances, 'good relationships' and a 'positive classroom climate' become firmly established. Less positive types of truce are also possible.

The main point for the present argument is that it is on the basis of such negotiated understandings, reached between teachers and children, that a sense of order, standards and justice derive in each classroom. A key aspect of this, and one which I would suggest can be used as a good indicator of the quality of teacher–pupil relationships, is that of 'rule-frame'.

The concept of rule-frame describes some key features of social understandings about behaviour which have been negotiated by the participants. Such social understandings are contextually dynamic. Thus, appropriate actions can be seen as varying, over time, in patterned ways, and with particular regard to factors such as setting, activity, phase of session and the people who may be involved.

There are five aspects of rule-frame which, I would suggest, are important to the overall quality of classroom relationships and these can also be seen to vary over time. The five aspects are: strength, content, breadth, consistency and legitimacy.

Strength is perhaps the most important aspect of rule-frame. If the rule-frame is strong in a classroom situation then actions are clearly circumscribed by social expectations. If the rule-frame is weak then more individualized actions are possible. Teachers can often control the strength of rule-frame through their actions. For instance, clear differences in children's responses are normally apparent when clear and emphatic instructions are given compared with casual requests. Children also often monitor teachers to diagnose their 'mood', for they know that a teacher in a 'bad mood' is likely to circumscribe behaviour tightly. With a teacher in a 'good mood' a bit more fun is possible.

A second aspect of rule-frame concerns the substantive content of rules. This encompasses the meaning and subject matter of the understandings themselves and is likely to have regard to such factors as time, space, movement, activity, noise and standards of work.

Closely related to content is the criterion of breadth. This reflects the range and comprehensiveness of understandings which have become established. This may vary and it is not at all unusual for a class or school to run very smoothly in all 'normal' situations only to be thrown out of gear by something unusual – a visit outside the school, a classroom crisis, a fire-drill.

A fourth dimension of rule-frame is that of consistency. This relates to the degree of variation in the strength or content of rule-frame over time. Consistency may be found in similar situations and in repeated activities over a period of time – or it may be lacking. A lack of such predictability is likely to be viewed negatively by children. The degree of consistency can also be studied within the phases and episodes of teaching/learning sessions. Thus a single session may move dramatically between periods in which behaviour is highly circumscribed and those in which 'anything goes', or it may, at the other pole, reflect relatively seamless continuities in behavioural expectation.

The fifth, and final, criterion which, I would suggest, can be usefully applied to analyse rule-frame is that of legitimacy. This is very important, for it provides a clear indicator of the degree and quality of teacher–child exchange in the establishment of behavioural understandings. After all, it is quite possible to conceive of a set of classroom rules being imposed by a powerful teacher which children have little option other than to accept. In such a case, the working consensus would reflect the power differential but would lack a negotiated moral foundation. It is thus perfectly possible for the rules and the rule-frame in operation in particular situations to be perfectly understood by children but for a degree of resentment and contestation to be present too. When rules are regarded as 'unfair' then their legitimacy is low. Where there has been open negotiation and rules are based on a recognition of the interests of the other, then understandings will be 'shared' and the legitimacy of rules, and of particular levels of rule-frame, will be high. The degree of legitimacy of rule-frame thus reveals the degree of acceptance of the content and application of rules.

This discussion has set out the conceptual 'tool-kit' on classroom relationships generated from a continuing programme of research into social aspects of classroom organization. It could be applied as a means of reflecting on processes in any classroom, both over time and within sessions. However, I want now to narrow the focus on to the issue of the content of rules and to consider this topic in more detail. As a means of doing this I will draw on data collected in one school – an 8 to 12 middle school in which I studied the views and actions of teachers and 11-year-old children over a period of two years[6].

TEACHER INTERESTS AND CLASSROOM RULES

Teachers have a very significant influence over the content of rules and, indeed, are important for children in a great number of other ways too. As Hargreaves put it[7]:

> The teacher is the immediate processor of the curriculum for the child. She is the evaluator of his academic work and assessor of his overall ability. She is the immediate adjudicator of his moral worth and the direct arbiter of the 'appropriateness' of his everyday behaviour. It is she most immediately and perhaps most significantly who therefore creates, transmits and attempts to impose definitions of the child as success or failure, ideal pupil or deviant.

I would suggest that this power of teachers can also be seen in the subject matter of the rules which they choose to introduce and maintain. In fact, I think that one can go further and postulate that the classroom rules which are most consistently promoted by teachers are those which relate closely to their own immediate concerns and 'interests-at-hand' in classrooms – they are rules, in other words, which enable teachers to 'cope' with classroom life[8]. In this part of the paper I will attempt to illustrate this contention with data concerning just four areas of teacher concern regarding children's classroom behaviour: that they should show 'respect'; maintain appropriate noise levels; work hard; and produce neat written work. This data is related to the teacher's interests-at-hand and thus this concept, in itself, requires some further clarification.

The concept of interests-at-hand stems from Schutz and refers to the immediate concerns which are felt by people through their direct experience of social situations[9]. The main interests-at-hand for teachers in classrooms are self, order and instruction[10]. Self, following symbolic interactionist tenets, is a primary interest and reflects a number of concerns such as self-image, workload, health and stress, enjoyment and autonomy. Order and instruction are what I refer to as enabling interests in that they provide the means by which the interest in self can be satisfied. Successful and committed teachers derive great personal satisfaction from their work with children[11]; however, few teachers can feel satisfied if classroom order is fragile or breaking down. Nor is there a sense of fulfilment if it proves difficult to help children to achieve appropriate educational objectives. In such circumstances self-image, workload, health, enjoyment and autonomy may all be adversely affected and teacher morale is likely to decline. There are thus very good reasons why teachers may wish both to introduce rules about child behaviour which will support their concerns and to negotiate so that they become accepted and regarded as legitimate. In the discussion of examples which follows, I will use interview data from four teachers to illustrate these points. These teachers worked in one tightly organized unit within the school and taught in what some people would regard as relatively 'formal' ways.

Showing 'respect' for teachers

That children should show respect for teachers was regarded as being very important by all the teachers who were interviewed and the most prominent reason given for this was the difficulty of 'coping' without it. For instance Mr Matthews commented:

> I think respect is *very* important. If you haven't got a certain degree of respect with the kids then it's very difficult to teach them or to cope with the discipline side of things.

A similar link between having respect and maintaining order and discipline was drawn by the other teachers and children were frequently reprimanded in ways which defined and enforced standards of respect.

In discussion of means of obtaining respect, Mrs Jones was particularly clear and forceful. She described the early process of establishment and her 'battle' for acceptable terms in a working consensus as follows:

> I would start off being very hard and having them in no doubt whatsoever about what I thought about certain situations . . . test sort of cases come up inevitably because you always get somebody who's willing to just push you that little bit too far, and they wait to see how you're going to react to a situation . . . and I think your reaction to that initially has to leave them in no doubt whatsoever . . . even if I found it amusing I personally would not let them see that at an early stage of the year because I think you're making a rod for your own back – it's different say by Easter because I'd know by that time that they would know where my boundary line was . . . so it's a battle won meaning that they don't need to test me to find out, they *know* without testing. If you establish your boundary lines, if you put them down firmly and squarely and stick to them as near as you can then they know where they stand, you know where you stand. Very often then if anything occurs, a look is enough from you to show your disapproval or whatever – they know how you're going to react before you even appear on the scene. Having established that, you don't need to keep on trying to establish it; if you don't establish that respect then that's what I'd call making a rod for your own back because you'd be constantly having to fight for control and telling them what is alright or not.

Each of the teachers described similar attempts to establish levels of 'respect' which were acceptable to them. In so doing the aspects of respect which they described were very close to the teacher–pupil relational rules identified by Hargreaves *et al.*, particularly those of obedience, good manners, permission-seeking and positive co-operation[12]. For instance, manners were something which, to quote Mr Matthews, 'we are always on about'. As he explained:

> It's very hard work upholding standards for manners and politeness, I mean you get some kids who just don't want to conform . . . or some who aren't used to it at home . . . or outside, or some that'll just try it on . . . so it's a constant battle . . . I don't think it's just personal opinions on manners that you're trying to get across it's just good manners in general. But personally I do think good manners are very important for the kids. It helps as well in the general sort of running of the place and making things easier for yourself if you haven't got them all running about or shouting out; if they know that they should hold the door open. . . . You don't feel then that

you're constantly going on at them because you can get that feeling and nobody likes it. I think it just helps in general . . . makes life a lot easier for you in any situation.

The concept of 'respect' seemed to crystallize the teachers' expectation of the children's deference to their authority over such issues and yet the teachers also recognized their own responsibilities with regard to fairness and consistency. For instance, Mr Matthews:

> Respect, I think, is gained through experience of handling situations so you can manage them well and be very fair, and through explaining situations and things that arise, and then being consistent. Children absolutely hate inconsistency, they like to know where they are.

It also became clear that, for these teachers of 11-year-olds, maintaining 'distance' was a significant means of both obtaining and sustaining respect.

> Mrs Jones: They meet you first as a teacher and I think possibly that first morning is the all-important one in so far as they are told in no uncertain terms that you expect respect for your position which obviously is as the teacher, that there are certain things which they will and will not do and I think in that respect I would insist on them respecting my *position* right from the word 'go'. If then along the way they begin to respect me as a person then that's smashing, that suits me fine, but I'd never let them get too close.

> Miss Newsome: [retrospectively] There are some that you feel closer to than others . . . but at the same time its far easier to keep some distance than to let it break down because then I think you have lost . . . if they start treating you like a friend or a sister or something like that then it's not on at all because that's when the cheek does come and you can see on occasions that they are overstepping the mark slightly with comments and that produces problems. Normally now I won't let myself get too friendly with them because I know what would happen afterwards . . . because then if they got a sort of situation in which they can say what they want, do what they want, then they're using you . . . they're manipulating you rather than the other way round . . . and you can't let that happen . . . you've got to keep it the other way round to survive. So I mean I'm not strict, I wouldn't say, by any means but I wouldn't want them to step over the mark.

In Miss Newsome's comments above, obtaining respect is once again identifiable in terms of satisfying teacher interests within a working consensus. It is a longer term, more stable, accommodation and deference in contrast to that obtainable by purely

authoritarian means. As such it is supportive of teacher interests
in the protection which it gives from discipline problems and in
the social status and esteem which it symbolizes and confers. As
Mr Taylor put it:

> It makes me feel more relaxed and in control if they treat me with
> respect. I feel awful if they seem to 'get on top' of me, and that can
> happen if I don't draw the line clearly about such things as respect
> and how to talk to me as a teacher. I like being called 'Sir' and
> things like the children holding the door open for me.

Noise levels

As with obtaining respect, the teachers felt that establishing
acceptable understandings about noise was important and was
something that 'you can never really forget about' (Mr Matthews)
and many censures of the children therefore stemmed from it.
Again, this concern seemed to be linked to personal coping in the
classroom and, with regard to this, I was able to distinguish three
aspects. First, certain types of noise were closely related to having
control and others to losing control, with dire consequences for
instructional objectives.

> Miss Newsome: If it's rowdy, raucous and hasn't got anything to do
> with what they're doing then it shouldn't be, but if it's a working
> noise it's OK. Very often there'll be a hum of noise and you'll
> look round and they can be talking about what you've set them
> to do, and as far as that's concerned then I leave them entirely
> alone, but if they're chattering on, and obviously taking no notice
> of what they're doing, then I don't think that's right . . . then I
> think they should get on. I think it's eerie if it's silent, but at the
> same time if there's a complete racket going on I'm utterly panic-
> stricken, I feel it's out of control.

> Mr Matthews: I myself don't like a lot of noise. If they start shouting
> across the classroom I stop it at once. I just think it's bad policy
> because obviously if they're shouting across the classroom they
> aren't doing what they should be doing . . . it comes back to
> trying to get into them that they are here to work as well as mess
> about . . . and that when it's a working situation then you do
> work.

Second, as Denscombe identified, noise levels were seen as
being important as an index for other staff of each teacher's
classroom competence[13]. They were thus a significant aspect of

each teacher's coping within the staff social system and of maintaining their autonomy. As Mr Taylor explained:

> If one particular class is making a row it's off-putting because you can hear what's going on, therefore I don't want to put myself in the same position so that someone else may be thinking 'Oh I wonder what's going off in there', – so there's that sort of pressure if there's much noise.

A third aspect of controlling noise levels emerged via the concern for order and instruction. When the class was noisy teachers felt a sense of unease and stress. Not only were facets of their self-interest under immediate pressure because of likely control and instructional problems but high noise levels also indicated more long-run problems associated with an unsatisfactory negotiation of a working consensus and a continuing threat to self. Mr Taylor again:

> If it's noisy I feel as if I'm losing control, it isn't very good then and it's very hard to regain a situation once the children have got away with being noisy a few times. It just drifts back every time if they don't really understand. Sometimes I have to get really cross. I might have to crack a book on a table or something, but if you don't have to say 'shut up' all the time then it's great, I feel really good, as if I'm doing the job well . . . and I enjoy it myself too.

In recognizing their need for the children to accept certain understandings regarding noise types and levels, the teachers also recognized their own responsibilities as parties to the working consensus, to be seen to act fairly as the primary arbiter. In particular, they identified the inconsistency of judgements which could result from their changing 'moods'.

> Miss Newsome: I suppose if you're in a pretty good mood it's far easier to cope with – to squash people and then turn round and make funny comments – the whole atmosphere is different if you're on top of yourself . . . but I think if you're under fire or something, then everything does build up and the slightest thing can be irritating and any noise, and anybody that isn't getting on can be a nuisance and a pest and be creating far more of a problem than perhaps they really are particularly. Sometimes I think you have to stand back from yourself and weigh things up and say . . . 'Am I being a bit too harsh today or . . . too easy going' you know.

'Getting on' with work

This teacher concern was a routine focus for the assertion of rules, particularly with regard to inattentive or evasive children. It most clearly related to what Hargreaves *et al.* called the 'lesson proper' phase of each lesson in which the teacher's instructional objectives are expected to be achieved[14].

> Miss Newsome: When the children are getting on, after you've started it off, then your next aim is for them to get on and produce something from it, and if they don't go through that stage then you're fighting a losing battle anyway so they've got to get on with work to achieve what's been planned . . .

'Getting on' thus represents the primary activity by which the teacher's enabling interest of instruction was intended to be achieved. It is therefore linked to coping via instruction. However, it is also directly linked to personal coping as a 'release' from immediate pressure, and as such was greatly valued by the teachers.

> Mr Matthews: It gives me a chance to relax, I'm no longer the centre piece as it were if they're working . . . it gives me a break – takes a bit of the strain off because it isn't easy controlling a situation so that it doesn't get completely out of hand. It takes the pressure off me and it means they're doing their lesson so it allows them to realize that they aren't here to mess about all the time, they are here to work as well.

> Miss Newsome: It releases me from them. If, having introduced what I want them to do, they can get on with it themselves, then it gives me time to go and pick up on individuals or do something that I want to do . . . it releases me from the pressure of the whole class . . . that expectation which they put on you – looking at you, waiting for you to tell them what to do, what to think about, them asking questions, giving you ideas – once they are set off by themselves you can think . . . right now I can go and mark a few books or pick up on one or two or wander round. If they're not getting on then you've got the pressure – why aren't they getting on? Is it because they can't do the work? Is it because they're fooling around? Once you've sorted that out the pressure's off slightly.

The last point made here by Miss Newsome raises a further aspect of the class's 'getting on' as a contribution to teacher coping, that of teacher competence and accountability.

> AP: Do you feel under any pressure to have a class that looks, or is, gainfully employed?

Miss Newsome: Yes. I mean obviously, if you look in on somebody else's class and they're either talking or they're obviously not interested in what they're doing or they don't appear to be doing anything then you think 'Oh I wonder what they're doing, what they're up to, I wonder why they're wasting such a lot of time' . . . and I feel pressure in exactly the same way . . . if anybody was to come into my class I want them all to appear as if they're doing something useful because if they're not doing something useful then it's clearly my fault that they're doing what they're doing . . . but obviously if they're here to do things, learn things, be educated then they ought to be doing it in some fashion whilst they're in the classroom situation.

Miss Newsome: If Mr Smith [the headteacher] came in I'd automatically think . . . 'is everybody doing what they're supposed to be doing'.

The teachers therefore attempted to set up situations in which the children would 'get on' as a means of instructing them, as a means of taking a break themselves from their ring-master role and as a means of maintaining an image of competence[15]. It is worth remembering too that child compliance with a teacher's request to 'get on' can vary depending on the nature and quality of the working consensus. If the children 'got on' willingly then the teacher felt well pleased.

Mr Taylor: I feel comfortable and satisfied when I can see them all getting on with something on their own. You know you must have set the lesson about right and I think if you get that it's very fulfilling – you get a good feeling. It's much better if you can get it like that.

If coercion was required teachers found it far less satisfactory.

Mr Taylor: Sometimes I have to keep them going just by making them – but the quality usually suffers and it's harder work.

Neatness

All the teachers from whom I am reporting here were keen on obtaining neatly presented work and this issue was a significant focus for the assertion of taken-for-granted understanding. Work which was not up to required standards was often returned to be rewritten. In one sense, the importance attached to neatness simply reflected an aspect of respect for the teacher and the teacher's personal preferences.

Miss Newsome: To me, if it looks neat and it's been thought about,
it's been done properly . . . if there's thought been put into it,
whether it's a load of rubbish content-wise, it shows to me that
they've been concerned about what they're doing. If it's untidy
then it automatically makes me think 'well if they can't be
bothered with it well neither can I . . . however, if you are continually making them do it again and again and again you very
often only get the same standard of work back and they're then
miles behind with everything else so the way round it as far as I
can see is to go around and make sure they're doing what you
want them to at the time . . . so I circulate . . . or I home in on
people who I know are going to be untidy in particular and I give
them all general rules about what I expect anyway as regards
margin and underlining and basic 'how to set things out'.

AP: Why do you want work presented like that?

Miss Newsome: Well it's for me, so it looks neat, it looks tidy. It's
been thought about carefully and as far as I'm concerned if they're
prepared to set it out neatly then I don't see why if one can do
it the rest can't do it . . . and it reflects the fact that I like it to
look neat and tidy.

However, neatness was not required merely because the teachers
liked the look of carefully presented work. Neatness had links
with instructional objectives because it tended to be associated
with higher quality and more careful work than would otherwise
be obtained. As Miss Newsome put it: 'It usually forces them to
try a bit harder'. It also had links with the coping requirement to
prove competence. For instance, Mr Taylor did not like 'other
teachers to see mucky, untidy work because it reflects badly'.

Of additional interest though was the way in which the insistence on neatness took pressure off the teachers. In the first place,
neat work took longer to do, so that less work was required to
be set and marked and less redirections of lessons were required.

Miss Newsome: It does take them longer, because if they're going
to scrawl then obviously it's quicker to scrawl than it is to write
tidily, and then I have to deal with it.

In the second place, the ease of marking was considerably
increased, again reducing the workload.

Mr Matthews: It takes pressure off me from the point of view of
when it comes round to marking and actually going over pieces
of work with children, or going over pieces of work myself. I
mean you know what it's like don't you when you've got piles of
books to go through and you get some kid's book and you think
– 'Oh God, no!, I can't face this one' – because you know, whether

that kid's tried or not, that it's going to be a right mess that book,
so it definitely helps in that respect.

Each of the concerns considered above – obtaining 'respect',
'reasonable' noise levels, a 'getting on' atmosphere and 'neat'
written work – was a frequent source of teacher censure and the
assertion of rules. Children would regularly be told to 'stop being
cheeky', to 'shut up', to 'stop looking about and get on' or to 'do
it again'. The prominence of such issues is most obviously caused
by their contribution to teacher coping. Rules about showing
respect and about noise levels related most directly to the teacher's enabling interest-at-hand of maintaining order, and through
it to the instructional enabling interest. Rules about 'getting on'
and presenting neat work most directly relate to the teachers'
instructional interest-at-hand but were also likely to assist in maintaining order and control.

Although each classroom and school situation is unique, I do
not think the illustrations above are atypical in representing four
common issues about which classroom rules are devised and maintained. There are many other important areas, for instance to do
with movement and with specific aspects of learning activities,
of classroom settings and session phases. Nevertheless, the four
examples do illustrate the important relationship between classroom rules and teachers' situational concerns. Of course, there is
also the issue, which I have left largely unexplored here, of how
children respond to such rules and seek, in turn, to influence
classroom understandings in respect of their concerns[16]. Here
though, I want to conclude by locating the analysis in a wider
social context and by considering the implications which may exist
for social control and social reproduction.

CLASSROOM RULES AND SOCIAL CONTROL

In what has now become a classic text in the sociology of education, Sharp and Green argued that classroom practice in a 'progressive' infant school in fact represented a new form of social
control[17]. The ideology of child-centredness was seen to obscure
an important teacher concern with the 'busyness' of children and
the use of a high degree of typification of children in terms of
their home circumstances and classroom behaviour as it affected
the teachers. In rather more theoretical approaches, both

Althusser and Bowles and Gintis argued that schools reproduce the skills of labour power and attitudes of submission which are necessary conditions for the reproduction of a capitalist social and economic order[18]. In the case of Bowles and Gintis, it was suggested that this was achieved through a 'correspondence' between the social relations of the workplace and those of the school.

Although such analyses are now regarded as being over-deterministic, they are important because of the issues which they raise about social justice. They are therefore issues with which many teachers are likely to be concerned. Furthermore though, since the question of the effects of classroom rules and relationships assumes a central place in such analyses, it is necessary to consider the question directly here. If we did not, it would be all too easy to assume that a demonstration of a humanistic concern for the quality of interpersonal relationships is unquestionably positive in its consequences.

Looking again at the views of the teachers in the case study school, it has first to be said that there were many indications of the teacher's awareness of the wider implication of their classroom practice. For instance, at the same time as the teachers stressed the importance of respect for easing their most immediate coping problems they were also well aware of links between that concern and external expectations. As Mrs Jones put it:

> You see our job is to teach, not necessarily to teach fact but to teach these children to be better adults eventually, we're a link in the chain that's aiming at this sort of acceptable level of . . . not necessarily intelligence . . . but socially accepted behaviour and all the rest of it, and learning to live by certain rules and . . . commonsense.

Miss Newsome also took a value position which had implications for deference:

> I think it's good for the children to have respect for adults anyway. I think whether its teacher–child, family relationships or just friends, you ought to respect people . . . whatever the relationship is. I don't see why you should expect anything other than respect and children to be well mannered and polite. I think it's all a case of getting on with people and knowing how to get on with them without causing . . . without being a nuisance.

The striking point here is that, although the first intention of establishing 'respect' derived from a desire to ease teacher's immediate coping problems, it had a second rationale in terms of engendering deference to authority *per se*.

Similarly, the teachers' intention of easing immediate coping problems by obtaining quiet, orderly classes can be seen as having potential macro-consequences. For instance, it is certainly the case that a requirement to be silent for long periods, which was a routine procedure in these particular classes, could be seen as alienative[19]. In combination with other routinized features of classroom life this could be seen as patterning personal development around the requirements of alienated work[20].

'Getting on with work' was seen to be important and to ease the pressure on teachers, but they also felt that helping the children to learn how to 'get on' was part of a 'preparation for life'.

> Mr Matthews: I think it's good for the children anyway – they have to get used to it.
> Mrs Jones: I think they've got to get on, I think that's very import-ant. They spend little enough time at school without wasting it chattering, there's plenty of time for that at playtime and dinner time and what have you, times that can be spent chattering or messing about but in lesson time they've got to get on. They've got to learn how to work without somebody constantly standing over them saying they must. If they're interested that's fine but there are times when they've got to get on with something that they're not as interested in. But I think that's a lesson for life, not just for school; when they go out and get a job of their own then they've got to be able to get on with things.

This last comment by Mrs Jones is an explicit statement of the link between school and work and the role of schools in preparing children for their future roles and workplaces.

Similarly, neatness was not thought of simply in terms of easing coping problems. It was seen as preparation for secondary school (Miss Newsome):

> Neat presentation helps them organize themselves. I think, they've got to organize their work in the secondary school into topics, into sections . . . in various ways of setting things out and I think it must help.

And as preparation for getting a job Mr Matthews:

> In a way it's a fact of life that there's more chance for them if what they do can be seen to be neat and tidy, I mean when it comes to filling in application forms and that sort of thing employers, if they get a form in front of them that's neat or that they can read and look at easily, they're more prepared to look at that one and at least consider it as opposed to chuck it out if it's an absolute mess – irrespective of content . . . and I think that . . . more than anything

else . . . is why I think it's so very important for them to be neat and tidy in their work *and* in their appearance.

Once again, in satisfying specific aspects of teacher coping pressures the teachers were simultaneously preparing the children for their future roles.

Interestingly, when the teachers were called upon to explain or justify classroom rules or standards, these were seen as being directly related to the instructional and disciplinarian aspects of teachers' socially ascribed roles. The value of such rules was thus taken for granted and 'made sense' both in everyday practice as teachers *and* in accounts as educationalists.

This last point links with one of the important characteristics of coping strategies. Hargreaves suggested that[21]:

> Although coping strategies are constructive and creative in character, nevertheless they are also based upon a set of tacitly accepted and taken for granted assumptions about schooling, children and learning.

He considered that such assumptions serve as 'parameters within which coping strategies are constituted' and represent 'features of a dominant social democratic hegemony'. Within such a hegemony a capacity for careful, industrious work and a 'sensible', 'responsible' demeanour are taken for granted and valued as commonsense attributes of the 'solid citizen'. Of course, in Gramsci's terms[22] 'commonsense knowledge' is characterized as a:

> mode of thinking which is an uncritical and largely unconscious way of perceiving and understanding the world.

The teachers' perspectives were certainly uncritical of what they viewed as their socially ascribed roles, and indeed they regarded them as having positive social implications. Of great importance though is the additional fact that such views were continually underwritten by the primary validity with which each teacher's daily personal experience endowed them.

So what does this argument amount to? It seems to me to be logically inevitable that what happens in face-to-face interaction in classrooms will have some consequences in terms of developing children's attitudes and, indeed, in affecting each child's sense of identity. We have seen evidence that teachers are well aware of this and are thoughtful about it. However, it can be argued that there is a tendency for such thinking to be so influenced by the practical necessities of classroom control and that this leads to an emphasis on particular values and dispositions rather than others. For instance, within democratic societies each citizen certainly has duties to contribute to social and economic development – a concern which has found full expression in the government statements which have led up to the Education Reform Act. However, citizens also have rights to voice criticisms, to exercise choice and to seek to influence policies. Such rights and freedoms are set out, for instance, in the European Convention on Human Rights. However, neither they, nor the understanding and skills which are necessary concomitants, are easy to provide for when facing the practical pressures and constraints of crowded and busy classrooms. In such circumstances it is all too easy to come to rely on a tightening of control and to avoid facing the question concerning the education of children to exercise rights as well as to accept responsibilities.

This argument thus stands as a note of caution regarding the commitment of both myself and many colleagues in primary education to the quality of classroom relationships. We have, first, to monitor our practice and reflect on the way in which benevolent intentions could manifest themselves as forms of constraint. Second, we need to consider the extent to which the children in our care are being prepared for citizenship as well as for work.

CONCLUSION

The Education Reform Act of 1988 provides a new context into which this argument must be located. If, as Tomlinson suggests, education is increasingly to be seen as a commodity, and schools are to be placed in competitive relationships with each other, it seems likely that pressure to provide demonstrable, tangible achievements will increase[23]. Thus, the emphasis at classroom levels on such qualities as neatness and 'getting on' with work may find a ready echo at the school level in terms of being able to produce evidence of pupil attainment. At both levels a pressure on tangible forms of productivity may come to be seen as the best, or only, way of coping with the demands of the situation. 'Good relationships' may well be seen as an important means of achieving such outputs and may thus continue to be given a high priority by teachers. However, this again raises the issue of aims, values and priorities – relationships for what? As I have suggested,

there is a tendency for 'good relationships', given the constraints
of classroom life, to become associated with control rather than
with enabling independent thinking and even critique. Of course,
to imply a simple opposition between such control and the degree
of emancipation which is sometimes promised would be far too
crude, but there is an undeniable tension between the two.

Teaching has never been easy and, in the particular context of
the new legislation, the issues associated with relationships, rules
and control remain a challenge for us all.

REFERENCES

(1) Alexander, R. J. *Primary Teaching*. London: Holt, Rinehart &
     Winston, 1984.
(2) Tomlinson, J. 'Curriculum and market: are they compatible?'. In
     Haviland, J. (ed.) *Take Care Mr Baker*. London: Fourth Estate,
     1988, p. 9.
(3) *See for a summary analysis* Pollard, A. *The Social World of the
     Primary School*. London: Holt, Rinehart & Winston, 1985.
(4) Sharp, R. and Green, A. *Education and Social Control*. London:
     Routledge & Kegan Paul, 1975.
(5) Symbolic interactionism: see Woods, P. *Sociology and the School*.
     London: Routledge & Kegan Paul, 1983.
(6) Pollard, A. 'Opportunities and difficulties of a teacher–ethnogra-
     pher: a personal account'. In Burgess, R. (ed.) *Field Methods in
     the Study of Education: Issues and Problems*. Lewes, UK: Falmer
     Press, 1985; and Pollard, op. cit.
(7) Hargreaves, A. 'The significance of classroom coping strategies'.
     In Barton, L. and Meighan, R. (eds). *Sociological Interpretations
     of Schooling and Classrooms*. Driffield: Nafferton, 1978, p. 75.
(8) Pollard, A. 'A model of coping strategies'. *British Journal of Soci-
     ology of Education,* **3** (1), 19–37, 1982; Woods, P. 'Teaching for
     survival'. In Woods, P. and Hammersley, M. (eds) *School Exper-
     ience*. London: Croom Helm, 1977.
(9) Schutz, A. *On Phenomenology and Social Relations* (ed. Wagner,
     H. R.). Chicago, USA: Chicago University Press, 1970.
(10) Pollard, A. *The Social World of the Primary School*, op. cit.
(11) Nias, J. 'Commitment and motivation in primary school teachers'.
     Educational Review, **33**, 181–90, 1981.
(12) Hargreaves, D. H., Hestor, S. K. and Mellor, F. J. *Deviance in
     Classrooms*. London: Routledge & Kegan Paul, 1975.
(13) Denscombe, M. 'Keeping 'em quiet': the significance of noise for
     the practical activity of teaching'. In Woods, P. (ed.) *Teacher
     Strategies*. London: Croom Helm, 1980.
(14) Hargreaves, D. H. *et al.*, op. cit.

(15) Smith, L. M. and Geoffrey, W. *The Complexities of an Urban Classroom*. NY, USA: Holt, Reinhart & Winston, 1968.
(16) *See* Pollard, A. *The Social World of the Primary School*, op. cit.
(17) Sharp, R. and Green, A., op. cit.
(18) Althusser, L. 'Ideology and the ideological state apparatuses'. In Cosin, B. R. *Education, Structure and Society*. Harmondsworth, UK: Penguin, 1971; Bowles, S. and Gintis, H. *Schooling in Capitalist America*. London: Routledge & Kegan Paul, 1976.
(19) Holly, D. *Society, Schools and Humanity*. London: Paladin, 1972.
(20) Bowles, S. and Gintis, H., op. cit., p. 147.
(21) Hargreaves, A., op. cit. p. 94.
(22) Gramsci, A. *Selection from Political Writings*, Vols 1 and 2. London: Lawrence & Wishart, 1978.
(23) Tomlinson, J., op. cit.

Chapter 7

Children's Perceptions of Teachers
Cedric Cullingford

EDITOR'S COMMENT

The image of the primary school shared by adults is a simplified one, but children also share a sense of the school's culture. Whilst they negotiate their individual ways through the rules and expectations of the school, they perceive its culture in a distinct and consistent way. Just as these parents later simplify their attitudes to what takes place in schools, so children first form a distinct impression, noting with precision what it is that makes schools, as institutions, unique.

At the same time children in schools know that behind such images there are crucial differences between schools, not so much in 'outcomes' as in the way they are run and the way teachers react to children. From their own experience they are not necessarily able to formulate what makes schools different, but they are able to understand, within the culture of schooling generally, what makes teachers different from each other. Children are aware that there is more to the experience of school than the accumulation of facts.

It is a great temptation to picture the role of primary schools as the passing on of information from one person to another, as if one could plan education like groceries; delivered and consumed. But it is a temptation not only for planners but even for some teachers to fall behind the notion of delivering the curriculum, of being imbued with subject expertise rather than human expertise; of knowing the facts rather than knowing the children. To many, prestige lies in knowledge of a subject, and they compare their social position to the greater status of their colleagues in other countries. But the same teachers know that the good teacher is one who understands how individuals learn, and enables them to do so.

The dichotomy between the status of knowing a subject and the ability to communicate that subject is also felt by children. And yet when we explore what children really think valuable we find that they do not see a good teacher as someone who only knows her subject. That might be prestigious but it is not valued. Children appreciate what good teachers are doing. They are not only affected by them, but know the difference they make. Some teachers enable children to respond; and that is where the heart of education lies.

Children also consistently appreciate teachers in terms of the processes of teaching and learning, in terms of skills and not just the attainment of knowledge. They acknowledge the abilities of teachers who show them *how* to do things, and not just what to learn. Of all people who speak for the importance of teaching skills the most powerful group are the 'consumers' themselves. ■   (C.C.)

Children develop a clear idea of the contrast between primary schools and secondary schools by the time they are preparing to transfer from one to the other. The picture in their mind is a universal shorthand which they all share and which reflects the way in which the two sorts of schools are contrasted, not only in how they manage the curriculum and organize the school, but in the role of teachers[1]. Primary school children share the view that secondary schools are more important, as well as bigger and more demanding:

> Girl: I think the comprehensive is the most important. Because that's where you get your 'O' levels . . . it's going to be a lot bigger, and the teachers are a lot stricter.

> Boy: The secondary school's more important than the primary because you've got more things to learn . . . There will be more classes . . . bigger children . . . bigger buildings.

In some ways the contrasts between primary schools and secondary schools are obvious. In primary schools children stay in one classroom, supervised by one teacher for the majority of the time. In secondary schools children go from class to class, to be taught by a variety of specialists. One result of this essential difference is that children associate primary schools with peacefulness rather than bustle, with calm rather than bullying and with close personal relationships rather than with impersonal rules[2].

Such a clear view of the distinct and seemingly obvious role of the primary school implies an equally marked view of primary school teachers. By contrast with the secondary school specialist, they are assumed to know everything and to be helpful in everything. But there does not seem to be the same respect attached to such helpfulness as there is to the teacher who is only seen occasionally and who is associated with one specialist subject. The view of the secondary school teacher, by children anticipating the experience, is of someone who does not pay them close attention.

> Boy: I don't think I'll do that at secondary school because she might be busy and say she can't help you.

> Girl: I don't think you'll have time to talk to the comprehensive teacher, because you'll be doing work and more work.

These teachers are seen to be 'strict' as well as distant, demanding more work as well as giving fewer explanations.

These anticipations heighten children's perceptions of the primary school teacher. They share a view which seems consistent despite different teaching styles. Underlying the teacher's various roles, children feel that the primary teacher is there to help, and support, and is willing to listen and explain. When children develop their sense of what makes a good teacher they often imply that the primary teachers stand, at best, for firmness of manner, ability to explain and friendliness. But as we will see, children do not necessarily *respect* those very qualities that they like. It's as if the very idea of the secondary school as a more fearful place, with bigger children, and bigger gangs, with more organized bullying, and with teachers so intent on their subject that they are indifferent to what takes place in the corridor, proved that it was more significant.

The very security that a primary school affords appears as being rather cosy to the children in their last year, as well as those in their first year at secondary school. The primary school is seen as altogether less demanding.

> Girl: it teaches you the basic things before you go on to the more complicated things . . . just the basic work.

> Boy: it sets you up for the secondary school . . . you're going to have to know about everything and there's a lot more subjects.

The primary school teacher, however, possesses particular opportunities because of the relationships which can be made. Many children respond to the idea of having the teacher as a friend.

> Girl: I think I would like to have one special teacher I could be friends with.

However, children also accept that the relationship with the teacher has a professional basis. What they hope for from their classteacher is a sense of personal interest and encouragement. When children criticize the ethos of the primary school classroom, then or subsequently they single out how much depends on whether they get on with just one teacher, and how difficult it can be if they do not. In secondary school they do not feel they have to get on closely with *any* teacher. But the rewards of a good relationship with a primary school teacher are clear.

> Boy: If I am worried about work I just go to the teacher and she helps me. If you get it wrong she shows you how to do it . . . and then she makes jokes and tells us how to do it.

> Girl: I normally go up and we talk about it and she shows me how to do it. She talks to the class as well. If so many people ask about one question she tells us all in a group. She says stop what you're doing and brings us up to the blackboard.

Children are also sensitive about whether they are liked or not; they want the teacher to 'look at you nicely' and to 'like everyone in the class'. With one or two exceptions they feel confident in their teacher because they feel understood and because they will not be rejected if they want help:

> Boy: I like to have one special class teacher because she's the one main one because she knows me better.

The teacher in the classroom creates a special relationship with both the class as a whole and with individual children. Within their classroom children feel a certain sense of security:

> Boy: I like to work in my own room as everybody is around you and you can hear people walking about and children talking and everything . . . I won't like moving from classroom to classroom.

> Girl: It's good being in the same classroom all day because you know where you are going and you get to know your classroom so you feel comfortable there.

But whilst the classroom itself seems secure, it is placed in the context of the school as a whole, and this conveys a far more authoritarian image. The teacher within the classroom might strike up a special relationship with the children, but remains the teacher, who represents a particular status and clearly defined organization. For children, school represents a series of rules, a code of discipline and a hierachical authority. Part of the security they feel derives from this sense of an imposed order. None of the children questions the need for rules. Indeed, they are adamant that on practical grounds rules are not only necessary, but become more necessary as they grow older. Without rules, children imply, there would be chaos:

> Girl: If we didn't have rules we could come to school any time we wanted. If we didn't have rules you'd get up to all sorts of mischief.

> Boy: If you didn't have rules in the school, everybody'll just be running riot . . . they may have some kids who turn out to be really naughty, so you'll need more rules.

Children accept the authority of teachers because they see them as part of the edifice of the school, as a place where there needs to be strict control, and clear organization. Teachers need to accept this fact about their position, even if they find it puzzling that children feel so strongly about it. They do know that they can only develop close and friendly relationships within the context of such authority. Children do not like teachers to break down the barriers of their professional status too far. Indeed, children sense the distinction between their own private lives and the kind of working relationships they develop with teachers:

> Girl: I would not tell my teacher because she is not part of my home
> . . . I don't feel I could go to any teacher if it was my own problem.

Children accept adult authority as more important than the authority of their peers, but they also accept the authority of their peers over that of adults who do not seem to them to justify, or carry out, the responsibility of authority[3]. Teachers are therefore seen in a somewhat ambiguous light. At one level they are appreciated for their willingness to be friendly, to convey a sense of humour, and to take seriously the individual learning difficulties of children in their classroom. But this is within the context of their status, and their role within the authority of the school.

Children's perceptions of what teachers should be like derive from a set of clearly formed normative values. They are based on expectations as much as experience and are shared consistently amongst them[4]. Children feel that teachers should be authoritarian, that they should make decisions and that they should impose order and structure. These are, of course, not the only values that children perceive in teachers, and the ways in which teachers convey such characteristics varies greatly. Nevertheless primary school teachers are seen as authoritative even if at a less exalted level that their secondary colleagues. Children respect the distance that they keep. They like to see consistency in teachers' behaviour, and this in itself implies a certain distance from children's individual needs. They do not like temporary teachers, partly because they do not know which rules have been negotiated and established. And children feel that they can get the better of teachers who become genuinely upset[5].

One of the essential tasks of primary teachers, which they carry out with great sophistication, is the response to *all* the children in the classroom. An experienced teacher knows instinctively whom to cajole, whom to ignore and whom to discipline when there is a sign of disorder in the classroom. But it seems that the teachers who are most closely aware of the needs of all the groups within the classroom are also those who have less highly defined authority in the children's eyes[6]. The most authoritarian created rules and expectations into which some children could not easily fit, even if they wanted to. For children appear not only to see the teacher's role as ambiguous, as a tension between the need for control and the need for responsiveness, but to develop such a tension in their personal attitudes to teachers themselves. They respect teachers as people who *know* a lot, and who convey information. They do not value teachers strongly as ordinary people, outside their role[7]. This is one reason why secondary school teachers have higher status in their eyes. It is as if the more that primary school teachers were appreciated for their openness and concern, the less closely they filled the prevailing sense of status. Mitman, for example, found that teachers who showed concern for the slower, less gifted children were both flexible and more accurate in their assessment of children's individual abilities and needs[8]. But these same teachers were also rated by the children as significantly lower in the quality of their teaching. It is as if quality of understanding and the ability to deliver information were not only separate, but somehow incompatible in children's eyes.

Children's views of the authority of the teacher include the acceptance that part of their role is the suppression of disorder. They are seen not only to represent authority but to impose it. Children need 'people to supervise them' and the people who do that, of course, are teachers; 'teachers are always there to tell you off and that'. The problem with children's notions that they do not have any *natural* tendency to behave well is that they force teachers into a role which seems alien to the children's interests.

Children assume that strict discipline is necessary but they also complain that there is not enough real knowledge of children and their work displayed by teachers. Whilst the children think that their *own* individual development is most important, the teachers rate staff co-operation as the highest priority. Children do not see much of the staff as a collective group, although they are assumed to be a coherent body, all fulfilling the same role. Instead, children are aware both of their own classteacher and the distinctions between one teacher and another.

> Boy: I don't like telling Mr J. when I'm crying . . . I had Miss H. . . . she was ever so kind . . . Mrs W. was horrible . . . she used to take it out on us.

Children's views of individual teachers are not normally so subjective. They are capable of giving a clear analysis of the teaching style, and more particularly, the teacher's attitude towards discipline. Teachers do not need reminding how acutely children observe them, and how children absorb clues from all the nuances of behaviour and language[9]. The very way in which children are spoken to reveals what the teacher is feeling and demanding, and children find it necessary to anticipate and guess what is being expected.

> Girl: If you're naughty she speaks deeply and when she looks happy she likes you. She always looks happy at me.

> Boy: After a while you know what the teacher's like, and you can go up and ask them and you'll know they'll help you.

> Girl: I'm quite happy here because Mrs P. likes me and she likes giving me responsibility. Thats how I know she likes me and she doesn't shout at me a lot when I've done something wrong.

The better the children are at guessing what the teacher demands, the easier they find it to accommodate to the tasks that are set them. This naturally means that some children are more adept at manipulating the circumstances to their own advantage than others. Part of the daily excitement of relationships between groups and the teacher in the primary classroom is the testing of the barrier, to see how far children can go in terms of independence or avoiding work, without causing the teachers to react. Pollard calls such children 'jokers': those who do not fit safely in the category of the obviously 'good' nor into the group which is definitely unco-operative[10].

The children who are best able to take advantage of the teacher

are the 'brighter' ones, who both make use of the resulting freedom and make the teacher feel rewarded because they guess what
is wanted[11]. Some pupils, therefore, have more power than others
over the teacher. Such power does not derive from increased
demand, for in the teacher's busy day, there is a sense of relief
when children are not insisting on too much help or too much
work. If children were constantly demanding more, teachers could
not always cope. It is as if the circumstances of the classroom
made it incumbent on all the children *not* to force the pace too
much, to allow for a steady work load that in the end suits both
the children and the teacher.

'Brighter' children show their ability to manipulate, to guess
what is wanted, and to please the teacher, even if they are not,
or perhaps because they are not, working too hard. Many of these
are girls. Boys and girls are aware of the distinction between
teachers' attitudes towards them in the primary school, even if it
is more apparent later. Just as children assume that they are all
naughty and need some form of discipline, so they notice that
boys are more frequently told off, and that they *need* to be. Boys
tend to initiate more interactions with teachers than do girls, and
this means that girls receive, in return, less response from the
teachers. But then boys also receive many more negative com-
mands and reactions that have nothing to do with work than do
girls[12]. Boys accept this as a consequence of their different behaviour patterns.

> Boy: Mrs Y . . . likes the girls. The girls don't get started fighting
> and swearing. Some of the boys get your nerves on edge and you
> get really mad and you start saying things to them or sticking your
> pencil into them. Miss normally lets the girls do things like give out
> the books or give out the papers . . . she looks angry at me. Some-
> times I'm in trouble. Some of the boys just make me get really angry
> and when I try to go up and tell Miss she won't even listen or the
> other boys try and stop me.

Whilst children are aware of the developing difference between
the sexes it is not something that figures in their attitudes towards
teachers as much as in secondary school. Nor do children indicate
that it matters to them whether the teacher is a man or a woman.
The characteristics of the good teacher are not dependent on
gender. When one boy remarks that he likes a 'man and a lady
teacher but I prefer a man' it is a reflection of his attitude towards

his home life: 'My Mum nags all the time . . . Ladies nag at home but not at school'.

The transmission of values, whether from the home, peer groups or school, is a complex matter. Teachers themselves use the way in which children see them, and their own roles, in a variety of ways. Whilst the ambiguity between their authority and their desire to help is at the heart of the way children respond to them, teachers find a variety of means to cajole children into working. They obviously succeed by taking on the attitudes and the policies of the school, standing for collective standards. But they can also withdraw from the institutional bias into a sense of their own individual expertise, or their own stated expectations[13]. They also recognize the ambiguity of their own role, just as the children experience it, as both part of a collective or group, and as an autonomous being. But, however hard teachers try to explore different kinds of relationships, and however hard they strive to create in children a sense of their own autonomy, they are faced with children's perceptions of them as people who control events. Children therefore see praise for their work as recognition that it is 'correct' and that they have discovered the way to please the teacher[14]. They also see criticism as referring to carelessness or lack of effort, as if the work set them were tasks designed for practice rather than for originality.

However hard teachers try, children will tend to interpret their 'open' questions which demand a variety of original responses as 'closed', assuming there is just one possible answer and that any other one is wrong. Children seem to think they are learning a fixed body of knowledge. They see the teacher as the authority who knows what this is. It is not surprising that children transfer their awareness of what teachers actually intend in matters or organization and control, to the parallel circumstances of knowledge[15]. Teachers use language in a distinctive way in the classroom, for instance with flippant remarks and insults, which are neither meant nor recognized as such and yet would be unusual if employed elsewhere. It is as if a different code were being used, like direct questions which demand nothing but 'closed' implicit responses. 'Could you open the door?' demands an active response, not a thoughtful consideration[16]. 'Do you know the answer?' means 'Tell me'.

Teachers' questions are perceived as purveying control and as far as the delivery of the curriculum is concerned, are assumed to be full of instructions. It is as if children assumed that the traffic of work were all one way; with them fulfilling whatever task the teacher wants, and asking the teacher only for help in carrying out that task. This is why it has been found that the teachers who actually ask most questions are least likely to receive questions back from the children[17]. Furthermore a battery of questions, far from stimulating children into spontaneous comments or any other contributions, can actually inhibit them from work. And yet questions have an important role to play, despite the suspicions of children. For children also learn information best when they are asked about it, not just because questions are a form of testing but because children, through the teachers questions, see the information as falling into a structure that the teacher is conveying in a subtle manner[18]. Questions are therefore not only seen as a means of conveying information but are used as a means of organizing information.

There is one way in which children feel that teachers can help; one gift that is especially appreciated. This ability goes beyond being friendly. It is the willingness and capacity to *explain*[19].

> Girl: I like more explaining. More simple. I get stuck and muddled. Then I try to work it out and if I can't go to Mrs G – then she helps me.

Most children assume that at secondary school it will be up to them to 'work' it out, but that in primary school explanations are clearly presented:

> Girl: Here they explain. They explain before they've given it to you; if you don't understand you get easier work to do.

This might be interpreted as a pupil's version of 'matching' but in fact children rate the desire to know and understand what they are doing so highly that it affects whatever work they are doing. They enjoy being challenged. They are willing to try new things but want to be able to get help, preferably from the teacher, although they also get help from their friends.

> Boy: We talk about the subject we are doing. If I'm stuck I put my hand up and she comes to my desk and shows me how to do it.

The willingness to be responsive to their individual needs seems to children to mark out the particular virtues of the primary school teacher. But the teacher is not only a responsive agent, waiting for clients behind the desk. She is someone seen as active in promoting clarity, and is often juxtaposed against the image of the purely distant teacher concerned that children 'get on with it' themselves by picking up information from books.

> Boy: I prefer doing it with all the class than just set from a book. The teacher does it on the board and writes things and everybody gets a chance to answer them. So its not like a book when you're the only one who can try to answer them. Everybody can do it and try and I like that better.

The primary class is, after all, a collective enterprise, where children also help each other. They know that as a central organizer the teacher makes sure they all join in:

> Girl: Instead of standing round the desk all the time and wasting time he reads out the answers. For marking. He gives us nice worksheets instead of using books all the time. He makes them up himself and that makes them better to do. He kind of puts them in his own words. It's easier as well.

Implicit in any analysis of work is the idea of the 'answer'; the correct response. This is true however the class is organized. The teacher needs to explain because the goal is to attain the right answer, or the right skill.

> Girl: When we are finding it difficult she talks a lot to the whole class. She doesn't always talk to one person, just when they go up. If about eight people keep doing it wrong she talks to the whole classroom.

The teacher is seen to balance the needs of the individual with that of the whole class.

> Boy: Well, she teaches the whole group and then she tells you on your own. She does work on the board . . . if you don't understand it you can go to the teacher and talk about it. If you're just lazy she'll tell you off.

Children assume that the teacher's questions are directed towards helping them know the information, and organize the information. The kind of teacher talk that children appreciate is not the general introduction, that seems to them to keep them waiting before they get on with the work, but the kind which is directed towards helping them understand *how* to do the set task[20]. The teacher is there to help them learn the *process* of work, and not just the information. Children are interested in learning the *skills* of work, and lay stress on the pleasure of being able to do the work, whilst understanding what they are doing.

> Boy: Learning your tables isn't fun but doing things is.

Girl: If you still don't understand you can go up to her . . . like fractions or anything you don't understand. Now I do because she does them again with you and shows you. Well, the teacher at the comprehensive might say 'well, you've heard me. Think it out for yourself. Sit down and carry on'.

The sense of dependence on the teacher is not so much as a conveyor of information as an explainer of *how* to go about work. When children talk about the curriculum they appreciate the work which seems to them active and engaging. They make a clear distinction between lessons where they are able to work by themselves in an experimental fashion and what they dismiss as 'writing'. One of the elements of the secondary school to which children look forward is the chance to do 'science' in a laboratory, with interesting experiments. What children do not like is 'doing the same things over and over again' or reading 'the same book so many times'. Interesting topics seem to the children to consist of activities, 'because you have to do things, like washing and cleaning and experiments'. Against this they feel that 'finding the answers is boring'. The sense of the *skills* of learning is clearly important to them.

Children are not afraid of having demands made on them. 'Easy' work is work they can understand. Once they know how to go about something they recognize the pleasure of doing so.

Girl: I like solving problems. You've got to think and work it out.

Boy: I like solving problems. Problem maths. You've got to use your brain and think and when it comes to problems I like working them out. I think the way you do things helps you to like it.

Children's pleasure in work derives from those moments when they understand the teacher's explanations and the task. The teacher is not just a responsive friendly person, but someone who is supposed to make their tasks interesting. Against the pleasure of doing work, like solving problems, children remember the many occasions when the work is undemanding, repetitive or obscure, so that they don't know *how* to go about it. There are many circumstances when children feel at a loss; not only when the teacher has not been clear, but when they feel held back by the lack of resources.

Boy: When I was in the infants we had the Ladybird books. By the second year I'd finished every single infant book they had so I had to go to the lower juniors. When I was in the lower juniors I finished all the books there so I had to get them from the upper juniors. In the upper juniors I nearly ran out of books. Because there was such a restricted thing and I found I was going ahead of everybody else.

The bright child might be able to use the circumstances better, but this is often because he is not making too many demands. The child who does stand out can be difficult to contain within the usual practices of the classroom. Often the work of school seems to children to consist of nothing but routine.

> Girl: I get fed up with English sometimes because we do English exercises and they are mostly all the same because they give you a paragraph of writing and you have to answer questions on it and we do that twice a week and it just becomes a bit boring. If they gave you a paragraph and if they asked you questions about it, then if they let you write it in your own words, kind of things would be better because at the moment you have to write it the same as it is for in the paragraph.

Children are demanding clients. They want all the work geared to their individual needs, and yet derive security from being in the class, working together. They assume that the teacher will know the answers to questions and yet give them the means to find them out for themselves. They want to work to the teacher's formula and attain help from the teacher and yet learn a great deal from each other. They *all* say that they like to work with a friend for their mutual benefit. They all expect the teacher to be fair and to know what is going on in the social tensions of their own peer group. They expect the teacher to be responsive, and yet see her as a distant authority. Most difficult of all, children, in discussing the problems of school, say that the most important question is the friendliness or the distance of the teacher[21]. And yet they also respect the most those teachers who seem to be most distant, most authoritative, and most associated with expertise in a particular subject.

All this put primary teachers in an ambiguous position. Children see the complexity of their role. It is as if the attitudes towards primary schools generally prevalent in society were already being engendered in the children before they leave. They already see the secondary school as more 'important'; not only because of the examination system, and the assumption that schools are there to prepare them for jobs[22], but because the teachers are experts within their own classrooms, on particular areas of the curriculum. The very ability of primary school teachers to create a harmonious working atmosphere, and to deal with a variety of different subjects, is both admired by the children and seen as only a stage towards the real work they will be undertaking later. The one aspect of the role of the primary teacher that children never quite forget, is the individual attention, explanation and concern. That is something children say they miss in the secondary school. But they are also quick to adapt. So they also associate the very virtues of the primary school with a way of life they later dismiss as belonging to the more comfortable years when they were young.

REFERENCES

(1)   The interviews on which this work is based were carried out with more than sixty children in four primary schools in the South Midlands. They were in their last year before transfer to secondary schools in which children were also interviewed. Each interview was extensive and covered a wide range of subjects, of which their attitude to teachers was one part. The children's answers were consistent on all the central points. It is only possible to give illuminative examples of what they said; but the examples do represent agreed positions. There was such consistency that one can generalize about what 'children' said.

(2)   Cullingford, C. 'School rules and children's attitude to discipline'. *Educational Research*, **30** (1), 3–8, 1988.

(3)   Lampa, P. and Turiel, F. 'Children's conceptions of adult and peer authority'. *Child Development,* **57**, 405–12, 1986.

(4)   Nash, R. 'Pupils' expectations of their teacher'. In Stubbs, M. and Delamont, S. (eds) *Explorations in Classroom Observation.* London: Wiley, 1976.

(5)   Davies, B. *Life in the Classroom and Playground: The Accounts of Primary School Children.* London: Routledge & Kegan Paul, 1982.

(6)   Tom, D., Cooper, H. and McGraw, M. Influences of student background and teacher authoritarianism on teacher expectations, *Journal of Educational Psychology*, **76** (2), 259–65, 1984.

(7)   Musgrove, F. and Taylor, P. *Society and the Teacher's Role.* London: Routledge & Kegan Paul, 1969.

(8)   Mitman, A. L. 'Teachers' differential behavior towards higher and lower achieving students and its relation to selected teacher characteristics'. *Journal of Educational Psychology,* **77** (2), 149–61, 1985.

(9)   Giles, H. and Smith, P. 'Accommodation theory: optimal levels of convergence'. In Giles, H. and St. Clair, R. *Language and Sound Psychology.* Oxford, UK: Blackwells, 1979, pp. 45–65.

(10) Pollard, A. *The Social World of the Primary School.* London: Holt, Rinehart & Winston, 1985.

(11) Sharp, R. and Green, A. *Education and Social Control: A Study*

in Progressive Primary Education. London: Routledge & Kegan Paul, 1975, p. 124.

(12) *See for example* Irvine, J. 'Teacher–student interactions: effects of students' race, sex and grade level'. *Journal of Educational Psychology,* **78** (1), 14–21, 1986.

(13) Pollard, A. op. cit.

(14) Pintrick, R. and Blumenfield, P. 'Classroom experience and children's self perceptions of ability, effort and conduct'. *Journal of Educational Psychology,* **77** (6), 646–57, 1985.

(15) Edwards, A. and Furlong, V. *The Language of Teaching: Meaning in Classroom Interaction*. London: Heinemann, 1978.

(16) Garvey, C. *Children's Talk*. London: Fontana, 1984.

(17) Wood, H. and Wood, D. 'Questioning the pre-school child'. *Educational Review,* **35** (2), 149–62, 1983.

(18) Wexson, K. 'Questions about a text: what you ask is about what children learn'. *The Reading Teacher,* **37** (3), 287–93, 1983.

(19) Goodnow, J. and Burns, A. *Home and School: A Child's Eye View*. Hemel Hempstead, UK: Allen & Unwin, 1985.

(20) Roehler, L. and Duffy, G. 'What makes one teacher a better explainer than another?' *Journal of Education for Teaching,* **12** (3) 273–84, 1986.

(21) Getzels, J. and Smilansky, J. 'Individual differences in pupil perceptions of school problems'. *British Journal of Educational Psychology,* **53** (3), 307–16, 1983.

(22) Cullingford, C. ' "I suppose learning your tables could help you get a job" – children's views on the purpose of schools'. *Education 3–13,* **14** (2), 41–6, 1986.

Chapter 8

Teacher Appraisal
Edwina Battle Vold and *Daniel A. Nomisham*

EDITOR'S COMMENT

It is a corollary to the existence of institutions that there should be appraisals of individuals, for established institutions imply the appointment of people to fit a hierarchy. Some cynics have suggested that the existence of institutions implies a constant restructuring, and therefore the need to make new and different kinds of appointment. But whether institutions are stable or not they have their own systems of appraisal, whether formal or anecdotal. There have been some notable examples of individual failures in a formal appraisal system through interview, like J. S. Bach. And yet the subject of teacher appraisal still strikes many as a new one.

Perhaps this sense of newness derives from the fact that any formalized system of appraisal is not dependent on anecdote but on a more time-consuming, and continuous, basis. It implies an ability to formalize opinions, and to have objective evidence to support them. Yet even this is not new. For years teacher training institutions all over the world have carried out 'clinical' observations, have subjected their students to meticulous appraisal, and have worked out in detail the means by which we can assess a teacher's performance.

What is new about teacher appraisal is that the focus is moving inevitably from the questioning of institutions themselves to the people in them, in such a way that new institutions will be set up to carry out such individual appraisal. If, as we know, one school can benefit children from similar backgrounds far more than another, it follows that one teacher can make more of an impact than another. What has always been understood on an anecdotal level could well become more openly recognized and, indeed, acted upon.

As the following chapter shows, there is both fear of appraisal because of its association with the negative business of trying to remove bad teachers, and a sense in which a clearer understanding of teachers' performance could lead to more support. In all aspects of the subject there is far more experience, both of the limitations and the opportunities, in the United States than in Great Britain. The material on which the following chapter is drawn has, quite clearly, universal inferences.

Rather like the impositions of national curriculum the matter of teacher appraisal has possibilities which can be used to advantage by the very teachers who at first feel most threatened. It could give greater understanding and therefore greater status to the teaching profession. It could give greater credibility in the eyes of parents, and even in the eyes of politicians. In addition, such appraisal, with its detailed analysis of actual performance, must imply greater communication between staff. Just as in the proposals for national testing, there will be a need for teachers to clarify their intentions in the classroom and diagnose the reasons for success[1].

There have been a number of studies on the different styles of teaching. Teacher appraisal, in its more sophisticated form, as the chapter indicates, could give a far more sophisticated analysis of individual performance. It could make us realize that the variations between teachers are not just a matter of style but a matter of personality. That realization could change the status of teachers. ■   (C.C.)

Teacher evaluation, sometimes known as teacher appraisal, has been a long-standing practice in American schools. It has taken varied forms over time and has served varied purposes. The misuse of the evaluation process has been much too frequent over the years. But there are more examples today in research studies and other professional publications of positive uses of teacher evaluation, and increased acceptability and approval of the process and its purpose. Evaluation can be defined as a process of gathering information for the purpose of decision making[2]. It is a process which allows one to make judgements about the worth and quality of a teacher or teaching. The process can be formative or summative in design, and collaborative or authoritative in its approach. When evaluation has as its purpose the identification or remediation of instructional weaknesses to bring about growth in professional behaviour, it is considered a formative evaluation. When its purpose is to make administrative decisions concerning the permanent appointment of temporary or probationary teachers, the reappointment of teachers, annual salary increases and promotions and in some cases the suspension of services of incompetent teachers, it is considered summative in design.

In many schools throughout the United States, teacher evaluation is used for either administrative decision making or for improving teacher performance and ultimately student achievement. In a research study done in Arizona in the mid-1970s this fact is aptly described. Of the 744 public schools in the state, 78.9 per cent responded to a survey regarding the evaluation practices. All of the schools conducted formal evaluations of their teachers; however, 56.1 per cent evaluated teachers for the purpose of improvement of instruction, while 45.1 per cent did so for administrative purposes[3]. Some school districts have used an evaluation process which combines both purposes without conflict.

In this chapter, we examine the various approaches to teacher evaluation or appraisal and the perceptions of those involved in the process. We also review the developmental stages in identifying criteria used in the evaluation process.

PERCEPTIONS OF THE EVALUATION PROCESS

Teacher evaluation is perceived as a positive or negative process based on how it affects a teacher's professional competence or security. Most teachers want to improve their teaching and do not generally object to fair evaluations. They want feedback about their teaching and opportunities to discuss what they do, why they do it and what other things can be done to help their students learn.

Most teacher evaluations in American schools are done by school principals or other supervisors who traditionally focus on things other than instruction. They seem to lack the necessary skills to give teachers the feeling that the evaluation process will be a valuable learning experience. Their perception of the process is that evaluation is an additional burden to an already busy workload. As such, the teachers who are products of the evaluation process are disillusioned. The response of a veteran elementary school music teacher in a small town in Virginia expresses this disillusionment with the evaluation process.

> He came in my classroom – stayed for about twenty-five minutes looking bemused and sometimes amused by the array of activity. I suspected that he had no knowledge of what I was doing or why I was doing it. Two weeks later when I read his evaluation of my teaching based on that one observation, I was convinced that my suspicions were accurate. The description of what I was teaching was much too simplistic, and the teaching behaviors highlighted were things which could have been done by any novel teacher or student teacher. My years of experience, my indepth knowledge of the field of music pedagogy or my teaching skills were not evident in his report. The ratings, though above average, revealed nothing of my competence.
>
> So what did I do? I signed it, of course. Just like I've done for the last eleven years. The process is a big joke. The principal does what he has to do, I do what I have to do to help him and then I go on with the business at hand – teaching.

This elementary music teacher sees the process of evaluation by her principal as meaningless and routine with no clearly identified educational purpose. The principal probably sees it as perfunctory and bureaucratic[4], providing sanctions for employment or dismissal[5].

Unfortunately, teachers sometimes perceive the evaluation process as an inspection process. This perception, which is not uncommon, produces fear and suspicion. Teachers who are fearful and suspicious do not risk showing weaknesses or entering into serious collaborative efforts to improve instruction or to enhance the learning outcomes of their students.

There are teachers and administrators, on the other hand, who perceive teacher evaluation as worthwhile and meaningful. They find the process helpful in the development of strategies for improving instruction and student learning. The process is non-threatening and the relationship with the evaluator is a shared and collegial one[6]. In most cases, these teachers have been involved in the total evaluation process, developing the instruments to be used, helping to establish mutually acceptable criteria. In an ideal situation, the teacher also is involved in determining the processes to be used in gathering data and how the data are to be used.

Teachers in the Charlotte-Mecklenburg School District in North Carolina perceive their teacher evaluation process as meaningful. It provides feedback to teachers about the extent to which they are meeting the performance expectations, which were co-operatively developed. It does not distinguish between evaluation as a means of improving practice and evaluation as a means of making personnel decisions[7]. Though the system is not universally acceptable to all of its constituents, it is a process that most teachers feel is fair and non-threatening.

Though not actually involved in the formal process of teacher evaluation, parents generally perceive it as a necessary process. Though often unintentionally, parents by their selection or deselection of teachers for their children inadvertently evaluate teacher effectiveness. Evaluation of teachers by parents, however, is not always unintentional. Because parents generally feel strongly about their children's education and their future, they hold all teachers accountable for what is taught and how well their children learn. In communities where parents have a strong concern for academic excellence, teachers are expected to adhere to academic rigour. Parents in these communities demand that administrative decisions be made as often as necessary to ensure that teachers who do not adhere to this criterion are denied tenure or promotion.

Parents generally have always demanded a degree of teacher accountability. During the 1960s, there were some large urban school districts and some small towns where there was total community control of schools. The parents and community were the decision makers regarding the curriculum, the materials and the teachers. They held teachers and administrators responsible for the lack of academic achievement of students and were visible and vocal with regard to the changes they expected for their children. In an address to Congress in 1970, President Nixon echoed this concern of parents. He stated that[8]:

> School administrators and school teachers alike are responsible for their performance, and it is in their own interest that they be held accountable. . . . We have, as a nation, too long avoided thinking of the productivity of schools.

Late in the 1970s, however, teacher accountability was de-emphasized. The problems in schools, the lack of achievement, the lack of discipline were attributed to the home rather than to the school and teacher[9].

There is a renewed interest in teacher accountability and thus a heightened concern for teacher evaluation today. Parents are demanding that school boards and administrators account for the quality of teachers they employ. Without moving into the type of community control of schools that characterized the 1960s and early 1970s, parents are demanding greater scrutiny of those entering the teaching profession and demanding evidence of reasons for initial and continued employment. This has led to greater use of teacher assessment or competency testing of those entering the profession and teachers already employed. A majority of states now test teacher competence in some way. They may test proficiency in language, teacher knowledge of specific or general curriculum content, pedagogical knowledge and technical skills. Some states have developed tests to assess all of the above. These competency tests, however, are surrounded by controversy and tend to separate the public from teachers, administrators from teachers and increasingly separate teachers from their peers.

Competency testing is not a panacea for improving instruction or for selection of quality teachers. It is only one variable which can be used to provide evidence of teacher potential and desirability. It should never be the sole criterion for hiring or dismissal of teachers.

Teacher evaluation is a necessary process as perceived by most teachers, administrators and parents. Its purposes are perceived differently by all constituents. Because of the differences in purposes and perceptions of the process, evaluation of teachers is engaged in with varying degrees of intensity and through the use of varied methods.

METHODS OF TEACHER EVALUATION

Several methods of teacher evaluation are used in school districts throughout the United States. Many of these methods are obsolete and provide little or no credibility to the evaluation process. However, many are effective and recognized for their strengths. These methods range from supervisory or clinical observation to self-evaluation. The method of teacher evaluation most widely used is supervisory observation.

Supervisory observation is a formal evaluation process. There are two parties of unequal status involved. Supervisors and teachers may jointly negotiate time and agenda, but the teacher is always aware that she is the one being observed and evaluated.

An essential factor in the supervisory observation process is that the supervisor is a disengaged observer who can see those things the teacher cannot[10]. Adding the eyes of a supervisor in an evaluation process increases the amount of data collected and both parties benefit from the identification of the teacher's strengths and weaknesses.

Supervisory observation usually done by a principal or a designated administrator has some built-in problems such as: (1) the presence of an observer; and (2) the selective perception of the observer. The presence of the observer can disturb the normality of the teaching/learning environment. The teacher will often show signs of nervousness and unnatural behaviour, especially when the observer is frantically coding or writing. The teacher commonly fantasizes the worst – that the observer is writing down all the bad things, so the lesson must be awful and the final evaluation will be punishment. The presence of an observer also affects students, especially when the tensions and anxiety are communicated through the teacher's nervousness and unnatural behaviour.

The observer is responsible for seeing, hearing and recording data which determine a teacher's fitness or competence. However, observers see, hear and record selectively. They are often impressed by different stimuli and because they have different degrees of familiarity with the subject area and different philosophies of teaching and learning, they sometimes provide a less than objective analysis of what they observe[11].

To provide a sense of objectivity to supervisory observation, many school districts rely heavily on rating scales or check-lists. These instruments are to provide a means of measuring the quantity or quality of teacher performance. Though widely used throughout the twentieth century the rating scale and the check-list have several limitations, one of which is that they tend to use implicit rather than explicit and clear criteria to measure teacher behaviour. One educator's description of rating scales is that they suffer from criterion contamination and/or criterion deficiency[12]. The following item taken from an actual rating scale used by students in teacher evaluation demonstrates how ludicrous this type of instrument can be in teacher evaluation.

The teacher encouraged me to learn.
Strongly Agree   Agree   Disagree   Strongly Disagree

The item on the instrument is vague and abstract forcing the user, whether student or supervisor, to read into the competency his/her own criteria. The result, is a 'halo' effect. A teacher liked by a student evaluator or a peer evaluator will generally be rated high while a teacher not so well liked will be rated low[13]. Rating scales or check-lists used during observation should reveal both strengths and weaknesses if it is a true assessment of teaching ability. However, rating scales and check-lists are not that objective. As a result, they are found to be unrelated to effective teacher characteristics. Though the rating scales and check-lists provide evaluators with some useful data, they are ineffective predictors of teacher effectiveness in that they are subjectively derived, vague in meaning and affected by the personal bias of the evaluators using them.

Other means of collecting data can occur during observations for evaluation purposes. Some school systems are utilizing script-taking, video-taping, audio-taping and instruments with more specific items or enquiries permitting the observer to focus and to attend to behaviour that both the teacher and the observer have collaboratively identified.

An increasing number of school districts are now using performance objectives as a method of teacher evaluation. This method has its roots in the one-time popular Education by Objectives (EBO), itself an off-shoot of the business-oriented Management by Objectives (MBO). It is also based on the contention that a successful teacher evaluation system must suit the educational goals of the school and management style of its administration. Using this method, the teacher, in co-operation with some other personnel, sets reasonable objectives and attempts to meet them. When the objectives are assessed or evaluated the findings can be used: (1) to motivate the teacher; (2) as a basis for rewards; and (3) as a guide for self-remediation and improvement. The performance objectives then represent the teacher's concrete 'job' description and the statement of the teacher's accountability for specified behaviours in a specified period of time. Discrepancy teacher evaluation is done to compare the teacher's performance *and* intended objectives with the outcomes. It is a form of 'horizontal' evaluation in which the observer critiques the teacher to determine the relationship between the teacher's intentions and actual behaviour[14].

Peer coaching is a method of evaluation used in many school districts. Its primary purpose is the introduction, maintenance or remediation of an instructional strategy. It is characterized by an observation and feedback cycle in an ongoing instructional situation. It involves a collegial approach in the analysis of a specific teaching behaviour.

Peer coaching has many functions and thus varied advantages. First, coaching provides companionship among peers. It can provide interaction with another during a 'learning process' where each participant can move through difficult stages with a professional colleague who is informed and supportive. Secondly, coaching provides technical feedback which helps teachers perfect identified instructional skills. The feedback, however, is non-judgemental. It is informative, constructive and productive. Thirdly, coaching involves application[15]. This part of the process helps teachers to find out what has been accomplished or how well they are doing along a continuum. This part of the coaching method is similar in purpose to discrepancy analysis in that the intent is to match behaviour with terminal objectives.

Many school districts (like Pittsburgh) are engaged in peer coaching as a part of the teacher evaluation process. It gives experienced teachers in the district the opportunity to practise different teaching strategies in a non-threatening environment and to receive feedback from colleagues. Usually the teachers in the Pittsburgh schools participate in a teacher centre where they attend clinics. In the clinics, observation skills are honed and skills in analysing teaching are developed. They learn how to provide feedback regarding effective techniques of teaching and how to offer peers they observe suggestions to improve weaknesses. Returning to their respective schools, the teachers take turns as observer and teacher. Through this process, teachers become conscious of the effective teaching techniques employed by others as well as themselves. The developers of the Pittsburgh teacher evaluation model believe it is an effective vehicle for improving instruction as well as for making administrative decisions regarding continued employment or deployment.

Another method of teacher evaluation used in many elementary schools in the United States is self-evaluation. Despite a widespread scepticism regarding self-evaluation, teachers and students do benefit. Self-evaluation helps teachers examine their teaching in terms of their behavioural characteristics, and in terms of the behaviours of the students involved. There is an immediacy and relevance in this method that is not characteristic of other evalu-

ation methods. This method of teacher evaluation is most successful in districts with self-motivated teachers who have a clear understanding of their personal goals and those of the school.

Two of the best-known clinical models of instruction are frequently used by administrators and supervisors for evaluation
purposes in American schools. They are the Madeline Hunter
Clinical Theory of Instruction approach and the Cruickshank
Reflective Teaching Model. Both have as their major purpose the
improvement of instruction: However, they provide a structure
for administrators and supervisors to use in formative evaluations
of teachers.

The Madeline Hunter Clinical Theory of Instruction[16] is one of
the most popular models used for teacher evaluation today. There
are few school districts that have not heard of the Hunter Model
and many are using or adapting parts of this instructional model
into programmes to improve teaching and teachers. The Hunter
Model, though not a method or a programme, yields a process for
identifying potentially effective solutions to instructional problems
regardless of the school's goals. The model originated in a laboratory school at UCLA resulting from many questions being raised
about how to produce a predictably 'good' teacher. What
developed was a clinical model that is generalizable, according to
its proponents, to all content areas and organizational patterns.

The model includes common elements which are identified as
useful in effective teaching. The elements reflect the psychology/e-
ducator background of its designer. They include: motivation,
reinforcement, practice, planning instruction, diagnosis and pre-
scription, expanding students' thinking, transfer, self-concept, and
retention. The lesson analysis, the conference and the coaching
are key factors in evaluating teacher performance. Though not
intended as a summative evaluation model, it is one of the most
widely used and widely abused 'methods' for evaluating teachers
in schools today.

The Cruickshank Model of Reflective Teaching[17] is a combination of self-appraisal and peer teaching. It is a form of simulation
which gives teachers the opportunity to teach and then reflect on
the teaching experience so as to improve in subsequent experiences. It requires a group of teachers who trust each other enough
to risk. It is a highly structured process with prescribed teaching
lessons. Because the content of the lessons is different from
normal academic subjects taught in the classroom, the emphasis

is removed from knowledge to process of instruction. The model, which takes teachers through four distinct steps, gives the teachers who participate time to think about their teaching behaviour and the opportunity to view others. This is an element of all 'peer teaching'. The ultimate goal of 'reflective teaching' is to help teachers to become more interested in self-improvement and self-appraisal.

Though the methods of teacher evaluation differ throughout the many school districts in America, administrators and teachers should adhere to some important guidelines[18]:

1. The method must suit the goals and the concept of teaching of the administrators and teachers.
2. The method of teacher evaluation should involve teachers in every aspect.
3. The method of evaluation must be perceived as meaningful and useful.
4. The commitment to a method must be endorsed by all involved.

CRITERIA USED IN EVALUATING TEACHERS

Historically, there have been many attempts in the United States to study the characteristics of effective teachers and to use those characteristics as criteria for evaluating all teachers. One of the most widely used studies was the Teacher Characteristics Study[19] published in 1960. The study, conducted by Kevin Ryan, had two basic uses in mind. One of these was an aid in identifying teachers who, at the time of selection for employment or in connection with promotion, had characteristic behaviours similar to those deemed important and desirable by a particular school system. At one stage the study consisted of a list of 500 critical behaviours of teachers. From the list, 25 effective behaviours and 25 ineffective behaviours were developed for use. The behaviours ranged from personal traits to instructional strategies. A partial listing of these behaviours follows.

Effective	*Ineffective*
1. Alert, appears enthusiastic	Is apathetic, dull, appears bored
2. Cheerful, optimistic	Is depressed, pessimistic, appears unhappy
3. Has a sense of humour	Overly serious

4. Is fair, impartial and objective in treatment of pupils	Is unfair or partial in dealing with pupils
5. Classroom procedure is planned and well organized	Procedure is without plan
6. Is clear and thorough in giving directions	Directions are incomplete and vague
7. Disciplines in quiet, dignified and positive manner	Reprimands at length, ridicules, resorts to cruel or meaningless forms of correction

There were other long lists generated by researchers based on new situations and new social behaviours. One such list was generated during a conference on superior teachers in 1962. A good teacher according to this list[20]:

Knows her subject
Knows about related subjects
Is adaptable to new knowledge
Understands the process of becoming
Recognizes individual differences
Is a good communicator
Has an enquiring mind
Is available
Is committed
Is enthusiastic
Has a sense of humour
Has humility
Cherishes her own individuality
Has convictions
Is sincere and honest
Acts with integrity
Shows tolerance and understanding
Is caring
Has compassion
Has courage
Has personal security
Is creative
Is versatile
Is willing to try
Is adaptable
Believes in God

These are desirable attributes for any human being but they are difficult to measure. There is also no evidence that these competencies are directly related to 'good' teaching. Other studies of teacher characteristics such as Flanders Study of Teacher Behaviors and the Minnesota Teacher Attitude Study yielded a list of teacher behaviours and were also used as a basis for effective teacher identification and for improvement of instruction.

Though criteria used in the evaluation of teachers vary within districts and among districts, there seem to be some common criteria found in all instruments.

1. *Competence in the subject area(s) taught.* Teachers are expected to be well informed and have a rich, extensive knowledge about the content for which they are responsible.

2. *Proficiency in oral communication.* Effective teachers use appropriate speech and are expected to provide clarity in the delivery of content and processes. They exhibit skill in questioning strategies, bringing students to higher levels of interaction and understanding.

3. *Proficiency in written communication.* Effective teachers are expected to be writers, proficient in responding appropriately to parents and managers and they are models for their students.

4. *Control of classroom environment.* The effective teacher is able to maintain classroom discipline. This discipline can range from extrinsic to intrinsic, from authoritative to permissive, from controlled to open, based on a teacher's philosophy and experience or that of an evaluator. It is one of the most frequently used criteria in teacher evaluation and one of the most frequently misinterpreted.

5. *Effective and appropriate use of instructional strategies.* Effective teachers are able to plan a lesson, teach a lesson, and modify a lesson based on instructional needs of students and the needs of the teacher.

6. *Competence in varied types of instructional technology.* Teachers are skilled in using traditional media, such as film, filmstrips, video-tapes and audio-tapes. They use information technology when appropriate.

7. *Recognition and acceptance of all students.* Effective teachers reveal through their verbal and non-verbal behaviour that each child has the ability to succeed and that each child brings to the classroom cultural and environmental attributes that make him unique and valuable.

8. *Emotional stability.* Teachers who are effective have a

sense of who they are and provide a sense of balance for their students. Teachers who believe they are effective, accept the responsibility for being effective. They value the profession and behave in such a way that peers and students also see value in them and what they do.

9. *Sense of humour*. Good teachers laugh with students. They are comfortable laughing at themselves and at situations, but never at students. This keeps the students alive and attentive and cuts down on the separation by authority and age[21].

10. *Professionalism*. Effective teachers are life-long learners who are constantly engaged in improving their skills and knowledge through continuing education, research and membership in educational organizations.

The attributes above are not guaranteed to bring about student achievement, which is the ultimate criterion of effective teaching. Why? Because they, too, are isolated characteristics that are subject to observer bias when specific indicators are not included to provide observers or evaluators with a basis for judgement. They also cannot be applied to all teachers in all teaching environments.

Isolating teacher behaviours has other drawbacks. What we isolate are the most simplistic teacher behaviours. These are teacher behaviours that are easy to observe and easy to measure. Teaching, however, is an holistic process. It is complicated. Its behaviours are so interrelated that isolating separate behaviours is not only impossible but undesirable. Another problem is that the behaviours usually isolated are the technical skills, which, as the elementary music teacher described, are skills any 'trained' person can have. Observing only the technical skills tends to ignore the emotional ramifications of teaching and the ingenuity that effective teachers have to invent dynamic patterns which create learning and excite students[22]. Evaluating teachers and teaching is not easy to observe or easy to measure. It is important that administrators and teachers engaging in the evaluation process seek ways to formulate criteria that best describe the technical as well as the emotional factors which may be observable but not always measurable.

SUMMARY

Teacher evaluation will continue its dominance as a process to help teachers improve their teaching and to help administrators make decisions regarding their teaching. There are three mandates for all educators involved in teacher evaluation:

1. Involve teachers in every facet of the process beginning with identifying the purposes for evaluation, designing the evaluation methods, and deciding what criteria will be used, who will do the evaluation and why.
2. There should be an emphasis on formative and collaborative evaluation rather than summative and authoritative evaluation to help eliminate fear, antagonism and disillusionment among teachers.
3. Though methods of teacher evaluation which stress the observation of observable behaviour will continue to be popular, there are those who believe that easy and observable is not necessarily best.

With support from research organizations, educators and psychologists, teacher evaluation can emerge from its stultified state into the future where effective teaching will be viewed as an art; where a teacher being evaluated will be able to create with less prediction, less control and with more imagination. It is a more difficult process to evaluate but a better way of describing what happens in a classroom where effective teaching takes place.

REFERENCES

(1) Galton, M. J., Simon, B. and Croll, P. *Inside the Primary Classroom*. London: Routledge & Kegan Paul, 1980.
(2) Welch, W. W. 'Curriculum evaluation'. *Review of Educational Research,* **39** (4), 429, 1969.
(3) Deever, M. R. and Berg, G. E. 'The teacher evaluation in Arizona and a proposed model'. *Reports on Educational Administration,* **6** (6), 1975.
(4) Wise, A. E. and Darling-Hammond, L. 'Teacher evaluation and teacher professionalism'. *Educational Leadership,* **42** (4), 28–33, 1984.
(5) English, F. 'Still searching for excellence'. *Educational Leadership*, **42** (4), 34–5, 1984.
(6) Jalongo, M. R. 'Decisions that affect teachers' professional development'. *Childhood Education,* **62** (5), 351–6, 1986.

(7) Schlechty, P. C. 'Evaluation procedures in the Charlotte–Mecklen-burg career ladder plan'. *Educational Leadership,* **43** (3), 14–19, 1985.
(8) Kimbrough, R. B. and Nunnery, M. Y. *Educational Adminis-tration: An Introduction.* NY, USA: Macmillan, 1976.
(9) Gallup, G. H. 'The second annual Gallup survey of the public's attitudes toward the public schools'. *Phi Delta Kappan*, **52**, 97–112, 1970.
(10) Goldhammer, R. *Clinical Supervision: Special Methods for the Supervision of Teachers.* London: Holt, Rinehart & Winston, 1969, p. 61.
(11) Ibid, p. 62.
(12) Cruickshank, D. 'Applying research on teacher clarity'. *Journal of Teacher Education,* **36** (2), 45, 1985.
(13) Champagne, D. and Hogan, C. *Consultant Supervision: Theory and Skill Development.* Wheaton, IL, USA: C. H. Publications, 1982, p. 61.
(14) Gitlin, A. 'Horizontal evaluation: its impact in three case studies'. *CCBC Notebook,* **11**, 3–13, 1982.
(15) Bauer, K. L. *A Comparison of the Changes in Teachers' Stages of Concern Regarding Peer Observation.* Indiana University, PA, USA, 1986. Unpublished dissertation.
(16) Hunter, M. 'Knowing, teaching and supervising'. In Hosford, P. (ed.) *Using What We Know About Teaching.* Alexandria, VA, USA: ASCD, 1984.
(17) Cruickshank, D. and Applegate, J. 'Reflective teaching as a strategy for teacher growth'. *Educational Leadership,* **38** (7), 553–4, 1981.
(18) Wise, A. E., Darling-Hammond, L., McLaughlin, M. and Bernstein, H. T. *Teacher Evaluation: A Study of Effective Practices* (Report No. RAND/R-3139-NIE). Santa Monica, CA, USA: Rand Corporation, 1984.
(19) Ryan, K. *Characteristics of Teachers: Their Description, Compari-son and Appraisal.* Washington, DC: American Council on Edu-cation, 1960.
(20) Combs, A. *The Professional Education of Teachers.* Boston, USA: Allyn & Bacon, 1965, pp. 2–3.
(21) Highet, G. 'The teacher'. In Yamamoto, K. (ed.) *Teaching: Essays and Readings.* Boston, USA: Houghton-Mifflin, 1969, pp. 82–3.
(22) Eisner, E. W. 'The art and craft of teaching'. *Educational Leader-ship*, January, pp. 4–13, 1983.

ADDITIONAL READING

Battle-Vold, E. 'Competency-based teacher education and normative re-education strategies for more effective inservice education'. In Grant,

C. (ed.) *Sifting and Winnowing*. Madison, WI: University of Wisconsin, 1975.

Bossert, S. 'Task group management and teacher control behavior: a study of classroom organization and teacher style'. *School Review*, pp. 552–65.

Brown, A. E. *et al.* 'Changing promotions criteria: cognitive effects on administrators' decisions'. *Journal of Experimental Education*, **52** (1): 4–10, 1983.

Buch, J. and Parsley, J. F. *The Way We See It: A Survey of Teacher Evaluation Policies and Practices Operant in the State of Washington*. Seattle, Washington: School Information and Research Service, 1973.

Hayden, E. T. 'Education as a state priority: five governors' views'. *NASSP Bulletin*, **70**, 11–19, 1986.

Hunter, M. 'Teaching is decision-making'. *Educational Leadership*, October, 1979.

Ishler, P. 'Upgrading education means upgrading teacher evaluation systems: merging of evaluation. An inservice approach'. Paper presented at the annual meeting of the Association of Teacher Educators, New Orleans, 1984.

Jacobson, P. B. *et al. The Principalships: New Perspectives*. Englewood Cliffs, NJ: Prentice-Hall, 1973.

Lysiak, F. P. A. 'A multifaceted approach to teacher evaluation'. Paper presented at annual meeting of the American Educational Research Association, Chicago, IL, 1985.

McCormick, K. 'Here's Carnegie's eight point action plan for transforming your schools'. *American School Board Journal*, September 29–30, 1986.

Monroe County Public Schools. *Teacher Evaluation Criteria*. Key West, FL: Monroe County Public Schools, 1969.

Natriello, G. 'Teachers' perception of the frequency of evaluation and assessments of their efforts and effectiveness'. *American Educational Research Journal,* **21** (3), 579–95, 1984.

Peterson, K. 'Methodological problems in teacher evaluation'. *Journal of Research and Development in Education*, **17** (4), 62–70, 1984.

Reilkoff, T. 'Advantages of supportive supervision over clinical supervision of teachers'. *NASSP Bulletin*, **65**, 28–34, 1981.

Rothberg, R. A. 'Helping teachers improve their teaching'. *Clearing House*, **53**, 102–3, 1979.

Snyder, K. J. *et al.* 'The implementation of clinical supervision'. Paper presented at the annual meeting of the Southwest Educational Research Association, Austin, TX, 1982.

Chapter 9

Teachers: Assessing and Assessed

Cedric Cullingford

> There's so much demanded of you every moment of the day you're teaching. . . . You've got hundreds of questions being fired at you all the time and so many things to think about and organize that you forget.

> You realize how isolated you are as a teacher.

These two quotations are taken from a series of interviews with experienced teachers who had served in schools long enough to be granted a period of time out of school for in-service courses[1]. They were asked to reflect on their time away from school, and also on what they felt about returning to the posts they had left. We often hear about disillusionment in the teaching profession, or the number of people who take better posts elsewhere. Indeed it is one of the significant messages, together with reports of the inadequacy of teachers' performance, that emerge from the reports in newspapers and journals. The sense of unhappiness with their lot, together with appreciation of the chance to get away from it, was expressed as consistently by the teachers in the survey as it is reported in the press.

It is fair to say that teachers have for a number of years felt unhappy with their status in society, with the lack of rewards both financial and emotional. But these pervasive feelings are not just temporary ones that reflect lack of pay or esteem. The changing role of teachers draws attention to the conflicts between the actual job and the community's perception of the job. In all the changes that we can delineate – appraisal, the place of others in the classroom, outsiders' control of the curriculum, more specialized roles, and responsiveness to parents – the teacher is left both isolated and yet responsible beyond the confines of the classroom. The tradition of the generalist teacher, employed by the state to overcome the deprivations of society, is being eroded, as well as the respect that went with it. Just as social workers were once automatically assumed to represent the state, in handing out largesse of cash and advice, and are now, in contrast, assumed to defend their clients against the state that pays them, so teachers' relationship with their employers is far less easy than it was. All these shifts of social emphasis have a consequence in the daily lives of teachers.

The two comments from teachers with which this chapter began sum up the tensions which are peculiar to the role of teachers. For many teachers the sense of the isolation of the classroom is paramount, both because of the complexities of what the classroom contains within its constrictions and because of the difference between this and the 'outside' world. Few people who are not teachers themselves can really share either the excitement of seeing children learn or the emotional strain that accompanies the difficulties. At the same time people outside the classroom assume they know all about education, having undergone it themselves. Not only do they feel that they know, but that they have a right to give advice, rather than rely on the professional judgement of the teacher. The 'demands' that teachers worry about are partly from within the classroom – the 'hundreds of questions' and the impossibility of appropriate individual attention, like marking in a class of thirty – and partly from without. Teachers receive a lot of generalized advice.

The difficulties of teaching are centred on the classroom; but this is also where most satisfaction is to be gained. And yet it is because of the disconnection between the isolated classroom and the overall educational experience that teachers can feel disgruntled. Classrooms are not really cut off from the world outside the school. All that takes place in them is related to the children's homes, their parents and their community. There are many reminders, even in the displays, of the encroachment of outside interests. The problem is that what happens to the classroom is not recognized by the context in which it is placed. Interest in results and in 'outcomes' is not fostered by an interest in the means by which they are achieved. Whilst teachers strive to convey the intellectual delight in helping children learn, they receive in return demands about what should be achieved in the curriculum, or in addition to the curriculum.

At any time of change in education we should not be unaware of some of the difficulties, as well as the opportunities, in the role of the teacher. In all the interviews carried out with teachers in mid-career, after years of experience, there was a sense of great relief for an opportunity of being away from the classroom.

> To be free of the burden that you always have hanging over you like a great black cloud; this class of children that you're responsible for, and you can never really get this out of your mind.

Anyone who takes their responsibilities seriously must reflect both on how much depends on them, and how little it is recognized, either by the children at the time, which is natural in the circumstances, or by others. It is therefore equally natural for the teacher to realize how large the gap is between what could be achieved, and what is. There are, of course, escapes from the sense of responsibility. It is possible to be less ambitious or to see teaching in simplistic terms as 'delivering the curriculum', placing all responsibility of learning on the recipients. It is difficult not to feel a sense of routine.

> I think this is one of the terrible things; when you've been teaching for ages you do tend to get into a certain style I suppose.

The burden of repetition is hardly satisfying, seeing yet another group of children move on. Yet the 'routine' is not like that of the articled clerk, or office worker. The 'routine' of the daily life of the school is that of constant demands, changes in plan, individual difficulties or traumas, and many interruptions.

> If you teach you're so busy you can't always think, I suppose.

Those teachers who were fortunate enough to have some time away from the classroom laboured under the disadvantage of having time to reflect on the daily demands they submitted to, year after year. Being given time to think and discuss major issues made them realize how little time they had in the normal course of events. Their return to the realities of the classroom could be traumatic, as if fulfilment had been consumed by survival.

> It's as if we'd been on another plane . . . and then the hard reality of the whole thing came back to you.

> You're full of zeal and energy and enthusiasm when you get back but after about three or four weeks you realize what the level's got to be.

The teachers who see the contrast between the difficulties of schools and the freedom of thinking about them draw attention to the most central tension to schools; the weight of expectations and the lack of time. Teachers long to reflect on what they teach, but are not given the resources to do so.

This sense of contrast is stronger at a time when some traditional attitudes to the curriculum are changing. There was a time when the curriculum was developed in an open partnership between parents, local education authorities and general expectations all interpreted by teachers. As an expression of a general view of what children should learn the curriculum was always being revised and scrutinized in an evolutionary way[2]. But the sense of autonomy between teachers and society has been roughly shaken, and the idea of consensus itself questioned. Instead of the diversity of local expectations and experiences gradually becoming a whole, we are now offered centralized controls with clear management and appraisals, with 'performance indicators' and 'bench-marks'. What schools have traditionally done well is no longer taken into account. What is of value is seen to be a clear set of objectives against which teachers can be measured. Instead of the tradition of the negotiated curriculum, and the concern for the individual child, we see the assumption that such tradition is a failure or misguided. The latent difficulties of the classroom are reflected in the arguments that underlie the Education Reform Act; the tension is between the individual privacy of learning and the publicity of results.

The presentation of a simplified view of the curriculum coincides, ironically enough, with the publication of many reports, including some by the government itself, that show that young children are more capable of advanced thinking than they have been given credit for, that they are able to analyse sophisticated matters in some depth and that many of the factors that affect their subsequent learning are more to do with emotions, relationships and motivations than with purely cognitive skills[3]. Whilst we learn about the realities of the human mind we appear either to ignore the evidence or act in a quite contrary direction. But this research is really the kind of information which teachers instinctively know about from their experience in the classroom. They might be offered simple views of learning by rote, but they know that what children learn is not the same as what is taught. They might be given simple views of child development, with various stages of incompetence, but they witness the ways in which children approach learning with all the sophistication and idiosyncrasies of adults. Teachers' awareness of children creates a tension between their knowledge of capacities and the difficulties in dealing with such knowledge. The tension is heightened when teachers' knowledge of children's learning is either dismissed or ignored for the sake of more simplistic notions. Thus, the sense of frustration at the attitudes of the state, or society as a whole, is a reflection of the tension implicit in the inner world of the classroom.

Even in the most smoothly run schools with a devoted and committed staff there are many points of tension. The number of studies that show headteachers under strain, or suffering from stress, seem to proliferate, even if nothing is done about the circumstances. But why should teaching be such a difficult job that even those who achieve success should be so unhappy? In studies of schools there is no doubting the peculiar and significant nature of the interrelationships of adults with each other. Indeed, one sometimes has an impression that children are there as witnesses of teacher behaviour[4]. We know that the more successful schools depend on fostering good relationships amongst staff, and sharing a common sense of purpose[5]. Teachers who continue to derive unmitigated satisfaction from their role are either protected from the insistent demands made upon them from outside or are so unified with their colleagues that they can confront the demands and even turn them to their own advantage.

Even in the best of schools, with high traditions of co-operation, there are particular points of difficulty, or tension. One school, which has for a long time had at least ten parents' evenings per year, many visitors to the school, an average of ten teachers' meetings per week, and a well-developed policy towards the curriculum, listed the points of tension. Some of these are outlined below.

Between integration and subject specialism

Organizing a classroom is always a matter of balancing individual attention with presentations to the class as a whole, defining work to be carried out by different groups of children, and working out the extent to which they can help each other. The 'standard' arrangement of a classroom, focusing on group work is itself a complicated matter, used in a variety of ways[6]. But the management of the classroom demands many skills, of understanding individual and group dynamics and the nature of learning. Can real learning be organized in terms of subject areas? One of the main traditions of primary education has been to foster a sense of the holistic nature of knowledge, expressed through general topics. But it is just this freedom to explore that has been most criticized. The HMI survey of 1978 pointed out how major areas of the curriculum were not being tackled, soon after the Bullock report stressed the need for *every* teacher to be a teacher of English[7].

Between telling and listening

The difficulties of finding time for each individual, to have a conversation with him, to mark his work, are obvious, and it is well known how little of a teacher's time is spent with individuals[8]. This naturally puts emphasis on the most traditional of teaching styles – the delivery of information. Schools will always be recalled by ex-pupils in their formality, and seen by children to be formal: this is because even if the teacher uses 'open' questions to which there is no rigidly 'right' or 'wrong' answer but a matter of opinion, children will still tend to assume that the teacher requires a particular answer, and will spend more time questioning what the teacher is after than thinking about the answer to the question. And yet teachers witness the way the children begin to grasp new concepts not by listening but by exploring ideas, by developing them orally or in writing[9].

Not having enough time to talk together and to think about what we are doing

There are always major issues to discuss, matters of principle as well as policy, and the main way that a sense of isolation is overcome is through meetings with other teachers. It is only by being given time to reflect that teachers can overcome this sense of surviving mitigated by staffroom conversations about experience. And yet it is sometimes difficult to convince those outside the schools that there is not only a wealth of material to think about, but that education *needs* to be thought about.

Between parents and teachers

Tension between parents and teachers varies between schools, and in some might appear to be minor. But there will always be some conflicts of interest, with the parent's concern with one child, against the teacher's sense of the class as a whole, between the interest in competition in which a child is placed in a rank order and the attempt to raise standards as a whole. Teachers welcome criteria-related assessment, but parents will still understand the concept of the norm.

Between experiences that have meaning for teachers and experiences that have meaning for children

The inner worlds of children are often unexplored and yet their success depends on their own perceptions. Rather than be sentimental about the optimism and openness of mind of children we need to know how the learning process can become more and more narrow, to beware of fitting new information into rigid attitudes. It is, in this process of unlearning, too easy to ignore the example that is being set.

Between needs and resources

Tension between needs and resources does not need much exploration, for the accommodation and equipment in schools, the state of the buildings and the availability of books all express what society as a whole thinks of its investment in education. Teachers find it is particularly galling that they are told on the one hand what they *should* be doing – attending in-service meetings for example – by the very people that deny them the resources to do so.

Lack of control in a number of important areas

Lack of control has been acutely felt both in small matters (whether to mend a leaking roof) and in large ones (like staffing appointments). It will also be felt in decisions affecting how to balance one against another, as well as in the lack of control over the curriculum.

Staff stress

We have already suggested that staff stress arises partly from the nature of the job, but is made far more immediate and widespread by the sense of being undervalued. Stress leads to staff absences; this in turn leads to heavier loads on the staff who are there. Some authorities replace sick staff only after several days, thereby creating more stress.

Lack of opportunity to involve colleagues outside the school in its development; insufficient dialogue with outsiders

The school day is such that a teacher is more than fully occupied all the time; it is also a very long one. By the time the displays are prepared and the equipment laid out in time for the children's arrival, and by the time the marking is done at the end of the day, let alone the preparation for the next day, the popular misapprehension that teachers only work when confronted by children looks singularly misplaced. And yet teachers need stimulation from colleagues, and need as many experts as possible from outside the school to help with curriculum development.

The difficulty in getting the local education authority to support initiatives

The larger the organization and structure, and the more the emphasis on accountability, the more pervasive the bureaucratic arrangements, it seems, which makes decision making very difficult.

Between the written intention and its actual performances

It is always useful to be reminded of this. To develop policies towards the curriculum, at national or local level, is comparatively easy; to make statements of intent is a facility many make use of. But the actualities of the classroom are often different. The teachers' own declared intentions are not carried out even as they try to do so[10]. But some official policies are impossible to carry out.

All these points are taken from one school in which colleagues spend as much time as possible in discussion. Their awareness of the tensions of teaching are not theoretical 'dilemmas'[11]. They are a mixture of the pressures of the job together with the many external constraints that are imposed upon them from outside bodies without thought of the consequences. And yet there will always be the compensations inherent in teaching, in doing a job that matters and that has consequences for other people. Real peace of mind depends not only on believing in what you are doing but in being encouraged to do it. Although the obvious encouragement seems little, teachers are also finding means, through their changing roles, to adapt to, and adapt, the constant changes. Teachers, after all, reflect the society they are in, as well as trying to form it.

Even in the proposals for assessment of the national curriculum there are signs of hope[12]. The arrangements proposed for monitoring and assessment *could* mean a greater chance for teachers to meet and articulate what they are doing. What began as a concern for broad testing could become a greater awareness of the importance of diagnosis and marking, and the time that they take. This, in turn, could lead to a greater awareness of the individuality of teaching, both for the teacher and the learner. The Task Group, after all, says that assessment[13]:

> could be an integral part of the educational process, continually providing both feedback and feedforward.

The question is how one finds time for such careful monitoring. Assessment can, in fact, be one of the most liberating of activities if it is designed to advise, support and help. That is, after all, what the phrase 'raising standards' should mean.

One of the ironic consequences of the plans to test all children, including the ages 7 and 11, is a greater awareness of the potential of assessment. The Task Group has suggested some significant criteria for the formation of assessment[14]. These would replace the traditional norm-related tests, which are based on the competitive urge to put all students into rank order for their own sake, as if superiority or inferiority were all that matters, as if it were necessary to have failures. Making assessment criteria-referenced could have a major impact on the way in which we see exams. The group goes on to say that assessment should be formative[15]:

> so that the positive achievements of a pupil may be recognised and discussed and its appropriate next steps may be planned.

This use of assessment, of constant dialogue, and constant concern to help the individual child could make an significant difference to the way in which a child's education is achieved.

But one of the potentially most significant assumptions about a nationally imposed scheme of assessment is that it should be moderated[16]. Moderation envisages two crucial matters: that teachers from different schools should meet to discuss the work of their pupils, and compare them with national criteria; and that 'teachers and parents (should) share a common language'[17]. The sense of isolation the teachers feel could be addressed and overcome if they shared ideas about the progress and attainments of children. It is by opening up the subject of children's learning that greater insight into the role of teachers could be made. The last of the suggestions made by the Task Group is that assessment should relate to 'progression'. Any good assessment scheme is not only diagnostic about what is wrong but suggests ways in which the individual can be helped. It might even suggest a coherent plan that covers more than one year.

The Task Group links assessment with the professional development of teachers[18]. There is a chance, given time and money, that some of the difficulties of the teachers' role could be overcome. When the Education Reform Act was first envisaged, with its controlling tendencies, the deliberate exclusion of evidence and its simplistic notions, it was greeted with distaste and suspicion, which did not prevent its being imposed. This being the case, teachers are showing not just that they can adapt to it but that they can *use* it to the advantage of education. Almost any measure, however arbitrarily imposed, can be made use of. The government's political decree that all schools should deal with the

economics of a 'free society' and explore the world of industry
has been used by teachers to explore the *nature* of the society and
the economy in a way that is not so superficial. Schools will
always reflect the nature of society, just as there will always be an
ambiguity about their role in society. But the school which feels
itself isolated is made use of by its community: whether it likes it
or not, the school which is aware of its community can make use
of it.

In teachers there is not only a great deal of commitment and
dedication but a store of potential creativity. In talking to teachers
one wonders whether their energy is really being used in the best
way, whether it is being turned to good use or turned inwards in
defensiveness. For those who had been on in-service courses the
return to the classroom could be traumatic.

> I thought to myself, gosh, when I get back to school I'm going to
> be such a whizz bang and make all the resolutions that I'm going to
> improve . . . (but) I felt I was speaking a different language from
> the rest of the class.

> It was quite traumatic . . . No one was interested to find out, to be
> honest.

The question remains whether, by greater communication of ideas
and common interests, teachers can feel more positive about their
role. The sense of isolation, and dedication to the classroom,
might have been enough to sustain teachers in the past. But the
changing role of schools and the changing attitudes to schools in
society force teachers to change their own roles. In all the pressures or tensions that teachers face the answer lies in greater
dialogue and greater co-operation, in making articulate and coherent what it is that teachers provide. If teachers could present
clearly what they do, to parents and governors and even to politicians, the sense of isolation would be eroded, and the very
people who seem most negative could see how important teachers
are. After all, they are all we have got.

REFERENCES

(1) These interviews were carried out before the Education Reform
　　Act, and were ostensibly concerned with teachers' views of the
　　usefulness of in-service courses, in promoting change in schools.
　　The views that were expressed in these lengthy interviews by fifteen

teachers reflected strong feelings which were not particularly sought in the interview. This probably lends their opinions more weight than if they were confronted with a series of questions about morale.

(2) DES. *The Curriculum from 5–16*. Curriculum Matters, HMI Series London: HMSO, 1985.

(3) DES. *Mathematics Counts* (Cockcroft report). London: HMSO, 1982; Speece, M. and Brent, S. 'Children's understanding of death: a review of three components of a death concept'. *Child Development*, **55** (5), pp 1671–86, 1984; Wells, G. *Language & Development in the Pre-School Years*. Cambridge, UK: Cambridge University Press, 1985.

(4) Nias, J. *et al. Staff Relationships in the Primary School*. London: Cassell, 1989.

(5) Mortimore, P., Sammons, P., Stoll, L., Lewis, D. and Ecob, R. *School Matters: The Junior Years*. Wells, UK: Open Books, 1988.

(6) Galton, M. J., Simon, B. and Croll, P. *Inside the Primary Classroom*. London: Routledge & Kegan Paul, 1980.

(7) DES. *Primary Education in England (survey by HMI)*. London: HMSO, 1978; DES. *A Language for Life* (Bullock report) 1975.

(8) Galton *et al.* op. cit.

(9) Söter, A. Recent research on writing: implications for writing across the curriculum. *Journal of Curriculum Studies*, **19** (5), 425–38, 1987.

(10) Vide Sharp, R. and Green, A. *Education and Social Control: A Study in Progressive Primary Education*. London: Routledge & Kegan Paul, 1975.

(11) Berlak, H. and Berlak, A. *Dilemmas of Schooling*. London: Methuen, 1981.

(12) DES. *National Curriculum. Task Group on Assessment and Testing: A Report*. By P. J. Black *et al.* London: HMSO, 1988.

(13) Ibid., para. 4.

(14) Ibid., para. 5.

(15) Ibid., para. 23.

(16) Ibid., para. 64 onwards.

(17) Ibid., para. 5.

(18) Ibid., para. 6.

Name Index

Subject Index